Thirsty for God

Matthew 5-7: Jesus' teaching for today

STEPHEN GAUKROGER

Scripture Union
130 City Road, London EC1V 2NJ.

First published 1991
by Scripture Union, 130 City Road, London EC1V 2NJ.

ISBN 0 86201 739 4

British Library Cataloguing-in-Publishing Data
A catalogue record for this book is available from the British Library.

Designed by Mark Carpenter Design.

Phototypeset by Input Typesetting Ltd, London.
Printed and bound in Great Britain by Cox and Wyman Ltd, Reading.

CONTENTS

Thanks to:

Becky, my editor, for her invaluable contribution to this book; SBC, for giving me the time to write and being the first audience for so much of the material; JLM, BJ, CE and SR, whom I love.

Dedicated to:

Fred and Muriel Wilson – special people who were among the first to make me 'thirsty for God'.

1

A NEW APPROACH TO LIFE

I would like to be able to write the best sermon in the history of the world but I am not sure that I am capable of doing that! So instead, I have written *about* the best sermon in the history of the world – the Sermon on the Mountain.

Matthew chapters 5, 6 and 7 are at the heart of the teaching of Jesus. As Jesus preached this sermon, something very interesting happened. At the beginning of chapter 5 we read, 'His disciples came to him, and he began to teach them.' But if we look on to the end of chapter 7 we find that, 'when Jesus had finished saying these things the crowds were amazed at his teaching.' The disciples were the first to come, but by the time the sermon ended there were crowds of people listening, riveted by what he was saying about himself and the kingdom of God. As news of Jesus' teaching spread, so more people arrived to hear him.

There were crowds of people hungry for the word of God, their spirits were thirsty for something that would really satisfy. And there are many people today with the same hunger and thirst. There's a lovely illustration here of how the church can help people find the living bread and water they are looking for. As you and I spend time with Jesus, perhaps together with other Christians, hearing his word and letting it change us, there will be others hard on our heels, wanting to hear it too.

IMPOSSIBLE STUFF?

When G K Chesterton first read the Sermon on the Mount he said, 'This is impossible stuff!' I'm glad he recognised that. Without the Holy Spirit living in our lives, its teaching simply cannot be lived out.

> 'Now when Jesus saw the crowds, he went up on a mountainside and sat down. His disciples came to him, and he began to teach them, saying:
>
> "Blessed are the poor in spirit,
> for theirs is the kingdom of heaven.
> Blessed are those who mourn,
> for they will be comforted.
> Blessed are the meek,
> for they will inherit the earth.
> Blessed are those who hunger and thirst for
> righteousness,
> for they will be filled.
> Blessed are the merciful,
> for they will be shown mercy.
> Blessed are the pure in heart,
> for they will see God.
> Blessed are the peacemakers,
> for they will be called sons of God.
> Blessed are those who are persecuted because of
> righteousness
> for theirs is the kingdom of heaven." '
>
> *Matthew 5:1–10*

It is important to note right at the start that Jesus' teaching here does not describe the way to become a Christian. Keeping the beatitudes will not earn us salvation, any more than keeping the ten commandments will. Rather, these sayings give a description of life *in* the kingdom of God, the way Kingdom people, who are *already* converted, are meant to behave. They describe the totally new approach to life and to God that comes with conversion. Our natures undergo a radical change when we are redeemed from the power of sin over us. In Jesus we have become 'new creations' (2 Corinthians 5:17).

The beatitudes are all about new attitudes working themselves out in new behaviour. They are the 'be-attitudes' – attitudes about being. They are all very practical – we should be-merciful and be-pure and be-peacemakers. If these attitudes are deep in our hearts, our behaviour will be that of God's children. It won't be 'impossible stuff' because it will simply be a matter of living in a way that fits our new nature.

A LIFESTYLE FOR TODAY?

Yet, this does *seem* an impossible way to live in today's cut-throat world. It might have been all right for Christians in the first century – people who knew Jesus first hand. But don't the pressures and demands of life today call for a very different sort of response?

I don't think so. In fact, when you think about the principles and values by which most people live today, I can imagine nothing more effective than the complete contrast of a life being lived according to the principles that Jesus set out.

Contrast this set of 'twentieth-century beatitudes' with those we have just read:

'Blessed are the pushers,
  for they get on in the world.
Blessed are they who complain,
  for they get their way in the end.
Blessed are the blasé,
  for they never worry over their own sins.
Blessed are the slavedrivers,
  for they get results.
Blessed are the knowledgeable,
  for they know their way around.
Blessed are the troublemakers,
  for they make people notice them.' *J B Phillips*

Well, you probably have some sympathies with that list! And all of us know people whom they describe perfectly. But there would also have been plenty of people in Jesus' day who would vote in favour of those principles rather than Jesus'.

The political situation

People in the first century who heard this teaching of Jesus were living under enormous stress. Israel at that time was like one big pressure cooker. The heat was on the Jewish people as they found themselves living under Roman occupation. They responded in four basic ways, just as we today respond to our own country's political structures and processes.

Firstly, there was the revolutionary response. The motto of one of the violently anti-Roman Zealot groups was, 'Let their blood be spilt in the streets.' Revolution would right all wrongs. They saw that the whole system was sick, full of oppression and injustice, and they wanted to get rid of it once and for all. Revolution was the only way to do that.

Then there were the escapists. A group called the Essenes felt that the problem was with the whole of society. The whole thing was so corrupt that there was no way it could be reformed. So they hived off to the desert and lived in their own community. They wanted nothing to do with the world. All it could do was contaminate them, so they separated themselves from it and left it to its own devices.

Thirdly, there were the compromisers – people like Matthew who took a job with the Roman occupying army and collected their taxes for them. The compromisers didn't think they could change anything and decided it was safest to 'play the system'. But they were seen as traitors by the other Jews.

Fourthly, there was the response of abdicating responsibility. This was the fall-back position of almost everyone in the ancient world. Basically, they had given up. 'How can we compete with this massive Roman army of occupation? It's just too much for us!' So their day-to-day lives were characterised by a kind of stoic acceptance: 'Well, this is all there is – what can *we* do about it?'

You will see these four attitudes in evidence during any general election campaign today. There are always a number of fringe parties who say that the election makes not one bean of difference – because the great revolution is coming soon and all these 'jumped up' politicians pretending to know what they're talking about will disappear overnight. And there are the escapists, who say they won't have anything to do with it;

the kind of Christian who washes his hands of 'the whole rotten business', isn't going to vote, isn't going to listen, doesn't want to know anything about it. 'No one has got the answer,' they say. Thirdly, it is easy to settle for compromise. 'Maybe that policy isn't very fair, but I don't suppose anyone has come up with anything much better – and anyway, it won't really affect me.' We can get so sucked into the world's way of thinking that we haven't a distinctive voice any more. Perhaps the most common response today, though, is apathy – abdication of responsibility. Whatever result comes out of a general election you can be certain that thousands of people entitled to vote didn't do so. They simply couldn't be bothered.

It was to people very much like ourselves, with the same sorts of scepticism, cynicism and idealism, that Jesus brought this teaching. It is just as appropriate today as it was back in the first century.

The voice of the church

Where were the Jews' religious leaders in all the people's turmoil – the equivalent of our national church leaders today? What help and guidance did they offer the people? Well, the Pharisees had locked up their faith in a traditionalism that simply had no power to address the issues of the day. They had nothing to contribute because they had not thought through the way God's people should interact with society and its political processes. They kept themselves largely separate from it, waiting for God to step in and change things for them, miraculously.

How does the church of Jesus in this country compare today? We are called to point people to the alternative values of the kingdom of God, by the way we live out its principles now. It is a kingdom that is already 'up and running' – it knows no beginning because it originated in the eternal God, and will know no end because Jesus' second coming will take it into eternity. Jesus' teaching in the Sermon on the Mount shows how we are to influence the kingdoms of this world for good, by the way we season them with the values of the kingdom of God. We cannot just sit back and wait for God to work a miracle – perhaps to make all politicians Christian, just and truthful overnight! Nor can we wash our hands of involvement in society because we dismiss the possibility of non-Christians doing anything really worthwhile. Jesus calls us to change our own attitudes first, by the power of his Spirit within us, and then to let the influence of God's kingdom values flow out from us to change and help our wider society.

EMPTY HANDS

When we are living for Jesus alone, our approach to life, its ups and downs, meaning and purpose, will alter out of all recognition. Our understanding of ourselves is the first thing to change, as we see ourselves for the first time from God's perspective:

> 'Blessed are the poor in spirit,
> for theirs is the kingdom of heaven.'

Over the years I have talked with many people before they have become Christians. Some of them find the decision a real struggle because they come to Jesus wanting to bring so much. They are so full of themselves: 'If I became a Christian, my word! I have this degree or that, this talent or that, I'm good at this or that; see how much I can bring to God! Wouldn't he be pleased!' Others have said, quite blatantly, 'I'd be quite a catch for God, wouldn't I?' And I've had to respond, 'Not really; no more than anyone else, because we can only receive all that God wants to give us if we come to him aware of our need of him. We need to come with empty hands.'

Augustus Toplady wrote a famous hymn which contains the lines, 'Nothing in my hands I bring, simply to thy cross I cling.' This is poverty of spirit; knowing that 'nothing good lives in me', as Paul said (Romans 7:18). It's those who recognise their poverty before God who will be blessed, says Jesus, because only they are really able to receive from him.

The basis of our Christian life has nothing to do with what we can bring God, but everything to do with what he brings us. It's not, 'blessed are the greatly skilled; blessed are the degree-holders.' Rather, blessed are those who come to God and say, 'Lord, I've nothing to bring to this arrangement – it's all on your side. All I bring with me is my sin, guilt, shame and failure, and I am asking in return for your life and love to fill me.'

It's a very one-sided operation! And it is vital that we realise this. After our conversion, the growth pattern in our Christian lives is dictated by our ability to recognise our continuing poverty of spirit. However baptised with the Spirit we are, however filled with his authority, however mature or spiritually gifted, unless we can see that without Jesus himself we are poverty stricken, arrogance and pride will soon settle into our lives.

There is a danger that, as we go on in our Christian lives, we can sometimes become arrogant. It's the feeling that, basically, we are better than others because God has used us or gifted us. We need to remember that we are made acceptable to God only because of what Jesus has done for us, not for anything we have done for God. The ground at the foot of the Cross is level. We are all equal there. We are all equally desperate, hungry for the saviour to reach and fill us. D T Niles, a famous missionary theologian, said that, when it comes down to it, evangelism is simply a matter of 'one beggar telling another where to find bread.'

There is an opposite danger too: we can become discouraged and dispirited because we *don't* seem able to live up to all that we think God asks of us. But Jesus says to us, 'It doesn't matter that you can't live a perfect life. Come with empty hands to me and let me clothe you with my perfection.' There's a song which puts it well:

> 'I am covered over with the robe of righteousness
>   that Jesus gives to me – gives to me;
> I am covered over with the precious blood of Jesus
>   and he lives in me – lives in me:
>
> What a joy it is to know
> my heavenly Father loves me so –
> he gives to me my Jesus;
> when he looks at me he sees
> not what I used to be,
> but he sees Jesus.'

The Cheam Fellowship

SPECIAL BENEFITS

When we live in the kingdom, living totally for Jesus, our approach to suffering will change, and we will discover some special benefits for his followers:

> 'Blessed are those who mourn,
> for they will be comforted.'

There is a special place in the kingdom for those who are hurting. The word Matthew uses is a general word meaning 'those who suffer pain and hurt'. He does not just mean 'mourn' as in 'bereaved'.

There is a story about an Indian woman who lived in a small village. Disaster after disaster struck her life. Eventually she went to the wise man of the village and said, 'I am broken and crushed. I have lost my husband and my son through illness and now I have no home at all. Life is so unfair, I want the gods to take it all away and give me a fresh start.' The wise man replied, 'All right. Collect a bowlful of fruits from all your neighbours. But you may only take a fruit from them if no tragedy has struck their household.' So the woman went round the village as she was told, and came back with an empty bowl. Then she understood that suffering, tragedy and pain, in different measures and in different degrees, fall into every human life.

As Christians we are not exempt from this, the common lot of humanity. This is not a very popular thing to teach. Most people prefer to be told that if they come to know Jesus he will bring them joy and happiness, and every moment will be filled with a blissful awareness of his presence. Like the sad Indian woman, we all prefer a god who will wave a magic wand and release us from trouble and suffering. Jesus didn't promise this at all. In fact, he promised the opposite. He warned that we are actually *adding* to our problems by becoming his disciples, because we are entering into spiritual conflicts too.

So why does Jesus say that those who mourn and suffer are 'happy' or blessed? Because he will be there with us in all our suffering, mourning, pain and hurt. He will not leave us to mourn and suffer on our own. Throughout his life Jesus showed that his concern was for the hurting, the destitute, powerless, the physically and emotionally crippled, lame and blind. Those who commit themselves to Jesus will have the special benefits of his love and strengthening. They will know they are infinitely precious to him and that he is able to turn all these difficulties into good. If you are hurting, whether through bereavement, pain or some other loss, the Jesus that we worship in our kingdom is specially sensitive to your needs; he loves you.

There is another way, too, in which kingdom people find special benefits in their suffering. Just as Jesus turned his focus outwards, to bring compassion and care to those who mourned, so his followers learn to minister in the same way to one another. The Christian community is designed to be a place of comfort and healing for those who are distressed. 'Love one another as I have loved you', Jesus said (John 15:12).

A LIFE UNDER CONTROL

When we live in the kingdom, the way we treat ourselves will change. We will be concerned to train and discipline ourselves in order to be able to do the work Jesus set before us – that of reclaiming the world for him:

> 'Blessed are the meek,
> for they will inherit the earth.'

In the French version of Matthew's Gospel, the word 'meek' is translated, 'debonair'. It's an interesting reflection on the gentlemanly nature of the word. The Greek carries the idea of being 'tamed': blessed are those who are tamed, under control.

If, like me, you're not particularly keen on dogs but tend to visit quite a few people, you will know what it's like to go into a house with a dog which keeps you constantly on edge. You sit on the edge of the settee or chair, looking out for it, imagining that at any moment it will be going for your throat! And you worry that if you move suddenly, even to shake your host's hand, you will find your arm bitten off at the elbow by a dog that is over-protective towards its master! Or you'll knock on the door, praying that the dog's out, only to hear a huge barking noise as it comes racing to the door. 'This is going to be another of "those" visits,' you groan.

Yet other people you visit may also have a dog but you haven't even known it's been there! It's not that it's locked up somewhere, it's just under control. When the owner says 'Sit!' it sits! That home is a much more peaceful place than one dominated by an animal that is simply out of control.

The same is true, to some extent, of our children, in that they, too, need to be 'tamed'. James Dobson, a doctor with many years of experience in working with children and families, writes of the need to shape a child's will without breaking his or her spirit. He speaks of this as bringing to bear a 'taming' influence on them. We've all been in homes where the children behave really badly. It's simply no fun to be there because the children are allowed to dominate everything. Their behaviour rules the whole household. Once you leave you breathe a sigh of relief!

Jesus' disciples are expected to have 'tamed' themselves, to have themselves under the control of the Holy Spirit. William Butler Yeats defined civilization as 'an exercise in self-restraint'. This self-restraint is to characterise citizens of the kingdom of God, too. Perhaps we need to be more careful about thinking *before* we respond to someone who goads us, or to hold back from instantly objecting, being angry or striking out. It is easy to 'open mouth and insert foot'! If we are aware of difficult situations that regularly crop up, or know that a particular person always winds us up, perhaps we could develop the habit of taking a moment to pray about our attitude and response before speaking. We should not be out of control but under God's control.

We need this self-discipline and training in order to be quick to hear the prompting of the Holy Spirit as he tells us how to respond in a given situation, or makes us aware of needs we can meet, or calls us to pray. Without self-discipline, no war is won!

RELEASING OUR GRIP ON RIGHTS

When we live in the kingdom, we will develop a new approach to other people:

'Blessed are the merciful,
for they will be shown mercy.'

There is a lovely gentleness in the word, 'mercy'. It is used 150 times of God in the Old Testament. In New Testament times it was usually used in the context of gladiatorial combat in the public arena. After a fierce and bloody fight a man lies prone on the ground, with a gladiator standing over him holding a sword or spear to his throat. The gladiator would look up to Caesar for the final word and if Caesar gave the 'thumbs up' sign the man would be allowed to live. If it was 'thumbs down' the man was to die. Perhaps the defeated combatant would cry out for mercy, and sometimes Caesar would stand up and say that, yes, he could go free.

Throughout the New Testament, 'mercy' speaks of a lack of revenge, the decision not to get my own back. In *The Merchant of Venice*, Shylock the Jew was determined to get all that he was entitled to from an agreement made with the merchant, Antonio. If Antonio could not repay by the set date the money borrowed from Shylock, he would forfeit literally a pound of his flesh. When it came to judgement, Shylock would not give an inch. He demanded justice. The judge urges him to show mercy, eloquently describing its true nature:

'The quality of mercy is not strained,
It droppeth as the gentle rain from heaven
Upon the place beneath: It is twice blest;
It blesseth him that gives and him that takes:
'Tis mightiest in the mightiest: it becomes
The throned monarch better than his crown;
His sceptre shows the force of temporal power,
The attribute to awe and majesty,
Wherein doth sit the dread and fear of kings;

But mercy is above this sceptred sway;
It is enthroned in the hearts of kings,
It is an attribute to God himself;
And earthly power doth then show likest God's
When mercy seasons justice. Therefore, Jew,
Though justice be thy plea, consider this,
That, in the course of justice, none of us
Should see salvation: we do pray for mercy;
And that same prayer doth teach us all to render
The deeds of mercy.'

The Merchant of Venice, Act 4 scene 1

Mercy is the opposite of the Shylock complex, the 'pound of flesh', 'pay me back' attitude.

How do you react when you have been snubbed and hurt by someone? Though we may not physically fight back, we usually want revenge! We are glad the person who made life difficult for us at work is overlooked for a promotion. We are secretly gleeful when a neighbour who has harrassed us doesn't get the limelight he wanted, or doesn't succeed at something or his children get a reputation for being trouble-makers at school.

Revenge is taken in more subtle ways in the 1990s than it once was. We no longer go round to someone's house and burn it down, but revenge is no less alive in the human heart. It is the desire to see other people openly put in the wrong, so that we appear to be justified. But we know that is not the way we are justified. Our justification comes about only through God's mercy. And in recognition of that, God calls those he has justified to show that same mercy and compassion to others.

2

A NEW THIRST FOR GOD

LONGING FOR HOLINESS

Another big change that happens in us when we come to know Jesus as saviour and lord is that our whole attitude to God changes. We can't get enough of him! And his concerns will become burning concerns for us:

> 'Blessed are those who hunger and thirst for
> righteousness,
> for they will be filled.'

Every time the phrase 'hunger and thirst' is used in the New Testament, it is used in the sense of hungering and thirsting for *some* of something – some of that bread, some of that wine. Except here. This is the only place in which it means, 'hunger and thirst for *all of it*' – not *some* bread, *some* wine, *some* anything else, but *all* of it.

I don't want just a little bit of righteousness, holiness, or of God's greatness – just the amount I can get away with – I thirst for all of it, to have it all in my life. If we are going to get anywhere in our discipleship, we must be filled with *all* of God's resources, not just a modicum or small amount of them.

Isn't that just like us as human beings – to be satisfied with a little, when God offers us a lot? Let's not be the sort of Christians who have had some of God's blessing but who will not cross the line of faith to receive more. There is still a wealth of things to experience beyond that which we already know. So let us ask God to awaken in us that hunger and thirst to be totally righteous and holy.

When the children come in at tea time and say, 'Mum, I'm starving!' we know they're not really. Probably not many of us have been at starvation point, desperate for food. The gnawing, aching hunger found in Ethiopia or the Sudan doesn't come in a week. It comes over months and years of having next to nothing. The desperation of that gnawing, empty pain is what God looks for in our spirits. Perhaps some of us are not more filled by God's presence, and not more fully anointed by his power, because our desire for it is only superficial. There can be a covering of complacency over our spirits; we are happy as things are. God longs for people who are desperate for himself, so that he can fill them with his Spirit.

BEING SINGLE-MINDED

Our thirst for God will spur us on to seek him out, to spend time with him, to discover what he wants done in his world and to figure out how we can fit into those plans:

> 'Blessed are the pure in heart,
> for they will see God.'

Purity is something we usually associate with the sexual aspect of our lives. Traditionally, a bride's wedding dress is white to signify her virginity. But the context here is much bigger. Jesus is talking about a purity or singleness of aim, being single-minded, doggedly pursuing a single goal without being deflected from it.

The goal Jesus speaks of is that of 'seeing God' – of bending all our efforts to know God and be known by him. The person who sets his heart on this will pursue God relentlessly! Knowing God will be the most important thing in his life and he will let nothing deflect him from seeking him out, talking to him, listening to him, growing in love and knowledge of him, and wanting to carry out his will. And Jesus assures us that if this is our aim, and we pursue it single-mindedly, we shall not be disappointed: 'they will see God'.

If we were all to start 'pursuing' God in this way, many of our churches would be revolutionised! House groups, worship services, decision-making meetings would all be transformed because we would have one common aim: to know God and make him known to others.

If we are honest with ourselves, we know that it is often other motives which drive us and make us decide for or against a particular course of action. Sometimes we are hurt by a cutting remark and our primary aim is to set the record straight. So we speak out in our own defence – and generally manage to 'do down' the person who dared to slight us. Or we feel we have been overlooked for some role in the church fellowship that we wanted, so we volunteer for another task – not genuinely out of a desire to see God's work done, but out of our need for recognition. And suddenly we find we are out of sorts with the world, with ourselves and with God.

We need to question our motives from time to time. But a word of warning: questioning ourselves too often and too carefully is a sure way to madness! We can never really get to the bottom of our motives; and because of our fallenness our motives will always, to some extent, be mixed. But we can usually become aware, without too much probing, of times when we are acting out of hurt, jealousy or fear. That's the time to be open with our brothers and sisters in Jesus and to let them minister to those needs. Then we will be more free to set our sights on achieving things for God's sake, rather than for our own. And, more importantly, we will be free to *be* the people he intended us to be, people who find their security in their *relationship* with him, rather than in *doing* things for him; people who are single-minded in their devotion to him.

Simon Stylites was a Christian who lived in Syria between about 390 and 459 AD. He wanted to be utterly pure in his devotion to God so, in order to prevent anything deflecting him from pursuing that goal single-mindedly, he lived in the desert on a twelve-foot square platform at the top of a tall pillar. He lived there for about thirty-five years. He may have achieved some good, but living like that was not what Jesus meant by being 'pure in heart'!

I know some Christians who misinterpret Jesus' words, though, in much the same way as Simon Stylites did. They think that being single-minded for God means that their lives should be dominated by 'religious' activity. They feel very uncomfortable about letting their children play for too long, or about wanting a lie-in on Saturday morning, going out for a meal, watching a video or playing a game of some kind. As soon as the thought comes that one of those activities would be rather nice, a little voice inside rebukes them: 'Tut, tut . . . this isn't exactly being single-minded for God, is it? I mean, how will sitting here watching Walt Disney achieve anything for the kingdom?'

Once, when I was in the middle of preparing a sermon, there was a knock at my study door, and I yelled out, 'Come in!' Nothing happened. So I yelled again, 'Come in!' Still nothing happened. That really annoyed me. It was so frustrating to be interrupted in the middle of prayer and study by some idiot – a deaf idiot at that, I thought. (It just shows how unspiritual we can be when we are being spiritual!) So I threw down my Bible, leapt out of the chair and ran round to the door wondering why this person didn't come in. I pulled the door open – and it was Bethany, my small daughter. 'Daddy, come in the house,' she said. 'No!' I replied. Then I thought, 'Now, Stephen . . .' and took myself in hand and gave myself a talking to for a minute. Then I invited Bethany into the study and spent a little time with her. I showed her some of the books as we walked round it and then I took her into the house and did spend some time playing with her. I was badly in need of a reminder that spirituality isn't always about high-powered stuff like praying!

Jesus' call to true spirituality is not a call to spend every minute of the day seeking God in prayer and reading the Bible. It *is* a call to make God the number one priority in our lives, and when that happens all these other things – watching films, going out, as well as prayer and Bible reading – will fall into place. When our overall aim in life is to please God and serve him, we'll soon discover that there are actually many, many ways in which he wants us to work that out in practice. God loves it when we spend time with our families! He is honoured when we are caring for them, enjoying their company and being happy with them. And we'll find that he provides us with the time for recreation and relaxation, as well as for the hard work needed in the kingdom of God.

POSITIVE ACTION

Our discovery that God is the thirst-quenching source of all that is best and most real in life, will make us want to share him with others. We will want our friends and neighbours to know, too, what it is to be at peace with God and with one another:

> 'Blessed are the peacemakers,
> for they will be called sons of God.'

I think this beatitude is one we can easily misread. We can think it says, 'Blessed are the peacelovers'. It doesn't! It is speaking of something much more active and positive. Peace*makers* positively bring peace where trouble would be the natural state. Peacemaking calls for hard work, patience and a sympathetic understanding of the grievances of the warring parties. Peacemakers long to see a unity of purpose and unity of activity among God's people. The idea behind the word is of those who 'make two into one'.

Again, this desire to bring about peace and harmony will mark out the Christian as someone different, because by nature we are all trouble-makers! Some of us love confrontation and conflict. We thrive on a good argument and love to tie someone up in verbal knots. We love it when there is a public disagreement followed by a good ding-dong argument. The tense atmosphere and distraught looks make for a good bit of real live drama! You might even feel specially gifted to take on the role of devil's advocate whenever there is a discussion in progress. At the office, at the house group, at the school parents' evening, you've always got to disagree.

Well, sometimes this is necessary; there are occasions when we do need to speak out and it is right that people should feel uncomfortable with what we are saying. But we need also to watch that we are not doing so simply because we like to be noticed, or want to show off our gift with words. To build people up is much harder than knocking them down. To make peace between two people who are suspicious, wary, or downright hateful of each other calls for a genuine commitment to the good of others. We will enable others to develop a respect for and unity with each other only at the cost of our own wishes and comfort.

We have already noted that peacelovers are not the same as peacemakers. Many people are afraid of conflict. They don't even like to disagree with someone, no matter how politely. Often, this is because conflict was handled badly in their family when they were children. As a child they would learn the signs of mother's temper brewing, and would scarper before the storm broke. Or, if they weren't able to get away, they would make themselves as small and unnoticeable as possible in order to try to avoid being hurt when she lashed out in frustration and anger. So now, when they sense disagreement in the air, all their instincts tell them to run, or freeze – at the very least to keep the peace at any price. And now they avoid talking about contentious subjects. But avoiding subjects that cause conflict, glossing over them or not letting people be heard, does not make for peace. It just prolongs for more years the agonies of untruthfulness, fear and unreality.

Peacemaking can only happen when two conflicting sides are brought out clearly into the open, and are encouraged to listen to each other fully. Sometimes we need to find healing and reconciliation for the emotional conflicts within ourselves before we can handle being in the presence of others in conflict. These hidden sources of our own fears need to be unearthed, brought to the surface and dealt with. This takes courage and a determination to enter into the fullness of the salvation Jesus has won for us – wholeness of mind and emotions, as well as of spirit. If this is your situation, your role as a peacemaker will be won only at a high personal cost, but will be all the more effective because of the additional insights and empathy your own struggles will give you.

Peacemakers are not content to let two Christians maintain a frosty, but polite, relationship. After the opening up of Eastern Europe in 1989, Lawrence Eagleburger, the American Under-Secretary of State, commented on a radio programme: 'One of the nice things about the cold war was that it was a time of stable relationships among the great powers.' 'Cold war', no matter how stable, isn't true peace, whether conducted between nations or individuals! The peace the Bible speaks of is not just an absence of conflict, but denotes a wholeness and healthiness of relationship. We are selling ourselves and each other short if we do not have the courage to live with the untidiness of growing, developing relationships.

God is good at creating things out of chaos. He calls us to go out of our way to *make* peace wherever there has been conflict, hurt, coldness or simply silence.

A RADICALISM THAT OFFENDS

Each of these 'beatitudes' captures an attitude that is different to those we normally come across, either in the way we relate to other people, or in the way we relate to God. In fact, the two are always linked. That is seen very clearly in the last of the beatitudes:

> 'Blessed are you when people insult you, persecute you and falsely say all kinds of evil against you because of me. Rejoice and be glad, because great is your reward in heaven, for in the same way they persecuted the prophets who were before you.'
>
> *Matthew 5:11–12*

Our world is under the influence of 'the ruler of the kingdom of the air, the spirit who is now at work in those who are disobedient' (Ephesians 2:2). Because of his influence in people's personal lives and in social and political structures, the whole tide of human thought and opinion is flowing his way. But when people meet Christ and surrender themselves to his will and his control, he turns them around to face the other direction. Slap bang into the oncoming tidal wave. Each of the beatitudes highlights an area of struggle, where the person who follows Jesus will find herself in conflict with the views of people around. But this struggle is proof of the reality of her faith.

Two misunderstandings

There are two common misunderstandings of persecution, or of what Jesus elsewhere calls, 'taking up your cross' (Matthew 16:24).

The first is the idea that whenever anything goes wrong I am being subjected to spiritual 'attack'. I might wake up with a headache, the kids are being atrocious, the boss at work is impossible, and when I run out at the end of the day, anxious to catch the early train home, I trip over something and fall flat on my face in a puddle. We all have days like that – it is part of being human! It is not likely to be anything more sinister.

The second misconception is to think we are being persecuted for being Christians when in fact we are being persecuted simply for being prigs. It's important to understand the difference! Some of us are so 'holier than thou' about our Christian faith that people are put off by our attitude, not by Christianity itself. If we go around with our noses stuck in the air, unwilling to get involved with them simply as people, we will find ourselves ostracised. This is not being persecuted for righteousness, it is simply being persecuted (and deservedly so)!

The real thing

The persecution Jesus meant is that which comes with being identified with his revolutionary new kingdom, and all that it stands for.

It is not something we know much about in the west, where it is understood that, within reason, we tolerate other people's beliefs. This attitude of tolerance was itself established largely through Christian concern and pressure for minority groups. Yet every country goes through times of hostility to Christianity. British Christians have been through them, winning the peace we now enjoy; and times of persecution will come again.

Persecution is very much part and parcel of Christian discipleship for many people in other parts of our world. Jesus seemed to regard persecution almost as synonymous with discipleship, because his disciples will find themselves swimming against the tide of their society's values and beliefs. What's more, having been 'born again' we no longer belong to this world or feel at home in it in the same way as before. We are essentially strangers here, foreigners – and we know how foreigners are generally treated by the indigenous population!

There is a hard question here which we need to face. If Christianity really is a radical call to be different, to be changed by the power of a living God who is totally involved in the world of the 1990s, why do we not experience more persecution in the west? I think it is largely because we have hidden the radical nature of the Christian faith behind a veneer of respectability. We have been more concerned to be acceptable to society at large than to be faithful to our Lord. So we have lost our cutting edge. We tell people what 'the church' says on this issue or that, and our national church bodies spend more and more time debating, discussing, and 'making statements'. It is much less comfortable, much more divisive, shocking and offensive to tell people what *Jesus* taught, and to stick by that. If we did this we can be sure that the theologians who are wheeled on to radio and television programmes to comment on moral or ethical issues would be the first to condemn our naïvety!

Are we prepared to face the ignominy of being considered simplistic? A bit fanatical? In today's culture the 'wise' person is deemed to be the one who accepts that truth is something no human can claim to have, so it is sheer bigotry that leads a person to evaluate one religion or creed against another. Christians involved in higher education, the media or the arts, are perhaps at the raw edge of persecution today. Their careers may suffer; they will certainly be regarded as simplistic and foolish – or that biggest of all crimes, intolerant – if they make it known that they are committed to Christ. The moral and ethical values that we must take on board as a result of this commitment run directly counter to much of the thinking of the powerful and influential in our country today.

Some questions

Here are some questions that we need to ask ourselves, also asking God to help us see if we are living as he wants us to, or if there is something we have missed:

- How many of the people you work with, live next door to, meet when out shopping, know that you are a Christian?
- As far as you can tell, what do they think it means to be a Christian? How accurate is their impression?
- How far are you helping to give them a true

impression of Christianity, by what you say, do, and what is important to you, and how far might you be hindering them in their understanding?

- How far does your life display the revolutionary nature of contact with Jesus Christ? Perhaps one of the reasons why we are not persecuted is that we have not yet grappled with what it really means to know Jesus. Go back over Jesus' teaching in these early verses of Matthew 5 and ask yourself how far you are putting it into practice. Where do you think changes are called for?

Blessed?

You may well be feeling the sting of persecution already. You may be made the butt of jokes at work because of your faith. You may have been passed over for promotion because you are not prepared to do the shady deals expected of you. You may have lost a job because you believed your church and family commitments are more important than working on Sunday. Or at home, you may find it hard to live consistently as a Christian if your husband or wife is hostile to your faith. Other family members too can bring to bear their own, subtle forms of persecution. You may find you are not really accepted by the wider family, because of your Christian faith. Perhaps they always treat you as something a bit 'odd' or weird – they don't really let you in to the family circle and relationships between you are cool. That can be a very hard and lonely sort of persecution.

So why did Jesus say we are *blessed*, or happy, when this happens to us? Well, there are some very good reasons!

- We are blessed because we are experiencing the same things that Jesus did. Jesus said that 'no servant is greater than his master' (John 13:16), and that if people hated him, they would not be too keen on his followers either. It is a real privilege to be able to follow in the footsteps of someone we love. We want to know what our daughter's first day at her new school felt like. Parents who lost sons in the Falklands war or in the Gulf war want to go there, to know a little bit of what it felt like to be there. It gives them a link with their dead son. It's something of the same with us – we want to identify as fully as we can with Jesus, and so we are happy when we can identify with his sufferings as well as his joy.
- We are blessed because persecution proves we are living out the full implications of the Christian faith. If we were not being effective in our witness and ministry, Satan wouldn't bother us and other people wouldn't feel threatened by our example. When persecution does come, don't let Satan's attacks get you down. Ask Jesus for his protection and keep your eyes on him. And when other people make life hard for you, don't hold it against them. That is your chance to show them what true Christian love is really all about!
- We are blessed because we will hear Jesus' 'well done'. We are not only rewarded now, in that our knowledge of Jesus is deepened through persecution, but we will receive a 'great . . . reward in heaven'. If you are being disadvantaged today because you are a Christian, be sure that the Lord has got saved up for you the splendours of heaven, the like of which you simply can't imagine!

3

SALT AND LIGHT

There's a lot of talk today about environmental pollution. Many people are very worried about it. But there's more than one way to pollute the place you live in. Someone has pointed out: '*You* are the environment in which other people have to live!' Other people have to live with our anxiety, grumpiness and outbursts of temper, just as they have to breathe the air around them. What sort of environment are we creating as Christians? One that's slowly poisoning the people around us, or one that's helping them to become healthier and stronger, spiritually?

Jesus calls us to be healthy influences on the people we meet day by day. Our lives are to have an effect; and to do that, they need to be different. I was talking with an industrial chaplain the other day, and he commented that the men he works with change their behaviour when he's around. Just the fact that he's there, and they know he's a Christian, makes them behave differently. Another friend of mine said, 'It's funny, but now I'm working full time in this office, people don't swear anything like as much as they used to.'

To explain how we are meant to influence society, Jesus took the images of salt and light. The Romans believed that salt was the purest thing there was, because it was made by the combined work of the sun and sea. Both salt and light can only do their jobs effectively if each is being fully itself. If salt 'loses its saltiness' – something that happened to an inferior sort of salt in Palestine, if it was left around for too long without being used – it loses its effectiveness. And the instant light gets tangled up with a bit of darkness – well, we have an indistinct half-light that's pretty lethal to drivers on the motorway! Jesus said:

> 'You are the salt of the earth. But if the salt loses its saltiness, how can it be made salty again? It is no longer good for anything, except to be thrown out and trampled by men.
>
> You are the light of the world. A city on a hill cannot be hidden. Neither do people light a lamp and put it under a bowl. Instead they put it on its stand, and it gives light to everyone in the house. In the same way, let your light shine before men, that they may see your good deeds and praise your Father in heaven.'
>
> *Matthew 5:13–16*

In many countries, salt is still one of the essentials of life. It was certainly essential in first-century Palestine: it was the most basic medicine, used for dressing wounds and stopping the spread of infection; and it was used to preserve foods, especially meat which would otherwise go off very quickly in a hot climate.

STOP THE ROT!

Donald Bloesch writes: 'We are called not to be the honey of the world but the salt of the earth. Salt stings on an open wound, but it also saves one from gangrene.' (*Theological notebook*, vol 1.)

Whether in healing or in preserving, salt is used to 'stop the rot'. In the same way, the church is called to be the preserver of values and standards in society, to prevent it from becoming so corrupt that it's useless.

What are some of the 'rots' in today's society that Jesus is calling us to work against?

The corruption of values

Margaret Thatcher will go down in history as the Prime Minister who campaigned for a return to 'Victorian values'. Now *I* certainly don't want to get back to Victorian values – to the days when you couldn't talk about table 'legs', for instance, and had to call them 'limbs' instead in case you offended anybody! Preserving values is not about going back to the Victorian era, but about going back to the Bible. The values Jesus calls us to preserve are God's values.

Many people today think there are no absolute values; we just make them up as we go along depending on what seems right for a particular society at any one time. Most of the time, 'civilised' people will make up rules that are generally good for people and are vaguely 'moral', or so we think. But the Bible tells us something very different: that there are some values that are absolute; they never change. They are the values that God holds, and that his people commit themselves to live by. We are to call our community and our world back to these absolute, unchanging values.

Many of the problems society faces today are here because we have ignored and abused God's laws. The results are predictable. If we think we can alter the law of gravity, so leap off a building hoping to land softly 100 feet below, we'll be disappointed! Pain will definitely be the result! If we break God's laws for living, pain in society results. It has done down the ages of history; it continues to do so today, because God's values are right for society.

The breakdown of family life

In a zoo, the lions, elephants, zebras and monkeys are all kept in separate enclosures. If they were all allowed to go wherever they wanted to, there would soon be disaster! At least, there soon wouldn't be any zebras, and the monkeys might not last too long either! God's laws build a strong fence around family life, not in order to make it restrictive and boring, but to prevent the people within it being attacked and destroyed by forces stronger than themselves breaking in. Selfishness, the desire for pleasure, the wish to be free of responsibility – these are all powerful pressures that will destroy a family if they are allowed in.

Family life needs to be kept strong and healthy. Where it is, society too will be happier and healthier. Where family life is under pressure from divorce, adultery and abuse, society itself begins to break up. We need Jesus' boldness to come out and say so; it's not a popular claim to make today.

Of course, we must not condemn those families that are suffering from breakdown. As well as Jesus' boldness to state the facts, we need his compassion for those who are hurting. Salt isn't meant to make a wound worse! It's put into a wound to help heal it. As grains of salt, you and I are sent into lives that are hurting, in order to bring love, warmth, support and practical care. When people talk to us about their divorce, or about a breakdown in relationships in their family, there's no point in pretending that it's all OK really. The divorcee *knows* the divorce wasn't, in itself, a good thing. It's not the best that God had wanted for that family. But we can also assure people that God continues to want the best for them and will not abandon them – certainly not just when they are most aware of needing his guidance and care.

We preserve society from moral corruption and social disintegration when we proclaim that God's standards are eternal and certain. That message won't be welcome; it will sting like salt in a wound. And so we must go on to bring people the good news that God loves them and longs to bring back to himself those who have fallen from the standards he has set out for us – and that includes all of us. He longs to bring us back to a glorious wholeness of life in him.

Materialism

Materialism is the other big 'rot' in our society. In its broadest sense, it means a greed for things, status, power or influence, that over-rides relationships and flattens values. It's the urge to 'get on' in the world at any price; to make a name for yourself. Suppose you've been offered a really good job three hundred miles away, with a big pay increase and a leap in status, but your wife or husband doesn't want to move house. Some people would size it up, then ask, 'Well, do I really need this person anyway? If she's not prepared to see how important my career is, I'd be better off without her.'

Materialism lives for the things that can be seen, and for personal pleasure. The big problem with it is that it has lost all sense of duty. Again, to say that we have a 'duty' to do certain things – to love our wife or husband, to put their interests before our own, to be honest at work – is to say something sharp, painful and unpopular. It's like salt in the wound. But without that salt sprinkled into their lives, our work colleagues, friends and family members will make decisions that will gradually destroy them.

Taking steps

What practical steps can we take to stop the rot in our society?

- Talk about God's values. People won't know what they are unless we tell them. When moral subjects come up in conversation, take the opportunity to say what you believe and why. Emphasise that it is what *God* says, not just what you say – and that's why you think it's important to take notice of it.
- Model God's values. If people see God's values lived out in the lives of their friends, it helps them understand those values better. Try to provide a model, in the way you live, of God's values: in your marriage, in your friendships, at work, in your use of money, and so on.

It is important to pick our own models carefully,

too. For example, if you are married, whose marriage do you model your own on? We need to adopt attitudes and ways of behaving that are really God-honouring, because our non-Christian friends will assume that the way we live is the 'Christian' way to live. Our words alone won't carry any weight unless they are backed up by our own lifestyle. As someone has said, 'I can't hear what you're saying, your actions are speaking too loudly!'

- Provide positive alternatives. Some Christians are so scared of doing anything wrong that they never do anything at all! Take Hallowe'en: it's not very helpful to go around saying, 'Hallowe'en is bad; you shouldn't have anything to do with it – and make sure your children aren't allowed to make witches' hats at school!' Instead, plan an exciting, positive alternative. Perhaps you could have a 'Family Carnival' on that night. Focus on angels or famous Christians. (After all, it is the evening before All Saints' Day!) Have lots of games and fun planned, and invite your non-Christian friends – especially those with children who might otherwise be going to halloween parties. Don't let the church be seen as something merely negative.

Do you belong to a local residents' association that holds its meetings at the local pub? If everyone usually ends up smashed it can be pretty difficult to know whether you ought to go or not. So why not provide an alternative: offer to host it at your home instead and lay on a good meal for everyone.

Alcohol is a real problem for many people. It's part and parcel of 'being sociable'. But non-alcoholic drinks can be just as varied. We have about ninety teenagers coming to a non-alcoholic cocktail bar at the Church on a Saturday night. Instead of commanding the local young people not to go to the pub (so guaranteeing that they will!) we offer a positive alternative: 'Hey, have you heard about this place? Come and play pool and meet your mates and try our "Gulf War Cocktail" (brown and horrible!).' We have a wide range of non-alcoholic drinks and are always expanding and varying the selection. We'll also throw in things like a 'Cocktail of the month' and the odd, tropical 'special'.

Creativity and imagination will help people to be receptive to the salt we want to sprinkle in their lives!

ADD SOME FLAVOUR!

Jan, my wife, is not a very big salter of food. So, when we have company, people often ask for the salt and they pour it on their meal with great abandon because it doesn't have the flavour they're used to or want it to have.

Jesus calls us to be the flavour of the world, to influence everyday life in a way that makes it more palatable for others. Perhaps we could create a better working environment in the office. Are relationships sour? Then they need the saltiness of a peacemaker. Is the atmosphere very competitive, people doing each other down in order to get promoted in their place? Model a servant attitude to others instead. Does everyone rush off as fast as they can at the end of the day? Show what it is to care about a job being finished well. Do your workmates read porn magazines at lunch time? Take your Bible in to read instead, or a Christian book, and talk to them about it. This is what it means to 'flavour' life. Or, to put it another way, 'We are the deodorant on the body odour of life!'

Getting out of the salt cellar

There's one big problem to this flavour business. We have to get out there! We have to be shaken out of the salt cellar into the world.

I'm sure grains of salt are much more comfortable and happy when they're with lots of other grains of salt, sitting minding their own business in the salt cellar. As Christians we like to do the same. All around the country, grains of salt get together Sunday by Sunday. They look around at each other and think, 'Well, here we all are in the salt cellar again; isn't it wonderful!' Then we all go home again in our little family packets, like the blue ones Smiths used to put in crisp packets. And once home, we only mix with our Christian friends, being salty with one another. Then, come Sunday, we all pour ourselves back into the salt cellar again; one great salty mob. 'Food', however, doesn't get a look in!

Jesus said that we are to the world what sprinkled salt is to food. So we need to get our there! We can be so concerned for our own purity that, though we might take a peek at the world out there, we rush back in quickly, in case we get contaminated.

At Stopsley, we occasionally pour out onto the streets in 'Make Way' marches. Yet these are little more than quick trips out of the salt cellar to look at the food, and then to come rushing back in again to safety. We have to do something more.

It's contact that counts. Salt is useless unless it comes into contact with the food. Salt doesn't just shout at the food from a distance, it gets thoroughly involved in it! So how do we make contact?

Use their language

I was in Oxford one day. Walking round the street corner I bumped into someone with a big black Bible, and he was preaching his heart out – or had been until I walked slap into him. I walked into him because I couldn't hear him, the noise of the traffic and of the milling crowds was so great. He stopped preaching momentarily and said, 'Excuse me!' somewhat surprised. 'That's fine,' I said, 'feel free!' And his friend gave me a tract. As I wandered off I took a look at it. Now, we *do* need people who are ready to take the message of the gospel onto the streets; it's very important that we are open with our faith. But what the tract had inside as its basic message was, 'He is the propitiation for our sins.'

If I asked you now to stop reading and to write down what that means, how would you get on? Some of you would say, 'Propitiation. Oh, yes! That's no problem – there's a subtle difference between that and expiation, and actually it's quite interesting that . . .' I guess most of us, though, would say, 'Propiti . . . what?' It makes me wonder what all those people in Oxford thought when they looked inside that tract.

That is not being salty in society. In fact, simply as an exercise in communication I would count it a failure. Of course, some people may have found Christ through that witness, and I would certainly not want to knock the commitment of the preacher and his helpers. But communication with other people has to be real. It has to be on their terms, in their language, with their dialect. The salt has to make contact with the food.

Go into their territory
Jesus was often found in places that 'religious' people didn't approve of. That's because he was looking for the people who needed God, and a bit of thought showed where he was likely to find them.

Similarly, if people are to talk with us at any depth, we need to be prepared to go to the places where they will feel relaxed enough to be able to do so. Sometimes, if a guy starts to share something with me but is obviously finding the church building or my office intimidating, I might say, 'Look, let's talk about this over a drink,' and we'll go across to the pub for a while.

Are there lots of keen footballers in your church? Well, do you really need to start a church football team? Why not suggest they join a local team instead? Is there a group of people talking about setting up a church photography group? Why not join a local group instead, or throw it open to the community as a whole and hold it on 'neutral' territory – the community hall or a local school?

We need to look for ways of making long-term contact with folk in our neighbourhood, if we are to have any effect on them as salt.

Restoring your saltiness

The mums you stand with as your children come out of school, the people you meet in the shops, office, class room or staff room – how aware are they that there is something different about you? How much are you flavouring the society in which you find yourself? I wonder if you have lost your saltiness, your ability to reflect to others what God has done for you? If so, there are some steps you can take to put things right:

- Tell God about it, and about how you feel. Ask for his help.
- Tell one of the church leaders about it, or a mature Christian friend.
- Do whatever flows out of that discussion:

  – Perhaps there is a need for repentance. Perhaps a coldness and hardness has crept into your relationship with God. That needs to be broken through.

  – You might just be going through a 'low' time and are generally run down and have no enthusiasm for anything.

  – Perhaps you need to get back into serious Bible reading and to set aside time for prayer.

  – Perhaps the problem is that you don't have a 'role' in your local church. We are only being salty when we are *doing* something. It may be that you cannot actually see any opportunities open to you; your church leaders should be able to help there. They can tell you what needs to be done and can talk over with you how you might best be able to help.

  – On the other hand, it may be that you *are* actually being salty in your community, you just don't *feel* that you are. Remember that saltiness is what we *do*. When Jesus calls us to be salty, he calls us to action.

DISPEL THE DARKNESS!

Some friends of mine were on holiday in Devon, getting

away from it all at a picturesque old farmhouse. In the middle of their first night there the wife had a coughing fit and wanted a glass of water. The husband dutifully found his way down the creaky, uneven stairs and into the kitchen. After a bit more fumbling he found the light switch and the place blazed into life – and the kitchen floor scattered in all directions as hundreds of cockroaches ran for cover! In mere seconds they had all melted away into the shadows. He didn't have the courage to tell his wife about this darker side of their holiday house until long after they'd left!

Light destroys darkness instantly, and sometimes shows up some pretty unpleasant things. When Jesus said, 'You are the light of the world', he might have had several things in mind.

Light and darkness cannot coexist

I worry about people who seem to want to be 'secret' disciples. Basically, they are committed to being Christians: they come to church, probably go to a house group mid-week too, but in their place of work no one would suspect they were Christians. Their discipleship is a secret one. Now that is a fundamental contradiction. It's like saying, 'I'll put the light on but I want it still to be dark.' Either our secrecy will destroy our faith, or our faith will destroy our secrecy. The two cannot live in tandem.

Yet many Christians try to live with this fight going on inside them. Some want the satisfaction and fulfilment of knowing Jesus, but they also want the comfort of not having to live up to his demands on them. If no one knows I am a Christian, perhaps I won't really have to change very much; the cockroaches can stay undisturbed in my life. But if I make too much of a song and dance about it, everyone will expect me to be some sort of angelic superman, always being kind, helpful and cheerful. And that's a bit much!

Jesus' words tell us clearly: 'You can't have both. You can't be filled with light *and* filled with darkness. You must choose to be either one or the other.' Nicodemus came to him by night, wanting to find out how to be a disciple but not prepared to be seen doing so! He found that to follow Jesus was going to make such radical changes in his life that he could not avoid being branded as 'one of them'. He had to make a clear choice.

Besides secret disciples, there are ignorant disciples! People who want to live a Christian life, but are secretive about it because they're slightly ashamed of what they believe. Others keep quiet because they aren't sure what they'd say if anyone asked them about it. That is basically a lack of knowledge. It can be cured easily enough by a long talk or two with other Christians who clearly *do* know what their faith is all about, or a visit to a Christian bookshop to find a book explaining Christian beliefs clearly. Don't let a lack of knowledge prevent your witness for Jesus being truly effective!

Light is visible!

D L Moody, the nineteenth-century American evangelist, said, 'We are told to let our light shine, and if it does we won't need to tell anybody it does. Lighthouses don't fire cannons to call attention to their shining. They just shine.'

We make our discipleship visible in two ways:

- By living for God. Our honesty, quality of friendship, reliability and care for others will all be noticed. The sort of neighbour, worker or parent we are speaks volumes about the revolution that has happened in our lives because we met Jesus. A constant, steady witness to this in the way we live is the only thing that will convince people that what has happened is not just superficial or some passing fad, soon to be given up in despair like the low-fat diet. Rather, this encounter with Jesus has been so stunning that it has fundamentally affected every area of my life. My home, work, career, morals, attitude – everything is coming under the impact of the gospel of Jesus Christ. Only a gospel with effects that radical will actually give the light that the world needs.
- By speaking for God. The fact is, we can't *just* do our work and assume that people will realise we are Christians. It is very difficult to do some jobs 'Christianly'. How do you type like a Christian? You just type!

It's a myth to say that if we only live the life people will start asking us questions. Some of us have been living the life for twenty years or more and no one has said two words to us about our faith other than something like, 'Do you go to church?' And we've even found that hard to respond to! There must be both life and speech if our Christian witness – our light – is to be visible. We have to learn to speak about God and the effect that Jesus has had on our lives.

Light guides

We need the light on to see where we're going. Just as the Bible is a constant light to *our* path (Psalm 119:105), so we are called to hold it up as a light for the rest of society.

Help people find the right path
If you've ever had a holiday in the Mediterranean you may have had the experience of going out for the evening to the local village taverna, quite sure you know your way around such a small place. And later on you start back on the ten-minute walk to your villa, gazing up in wonder at the amazing assortment of stars sprinkled about in the sky. After you've been walking a while you begin to wonder why you aren't recognising the path – but then, it is pitch black now, and everything does look different at night. But half an hour later you're still trying to figure out exactly where you are – all these houses with shutters and little low walls look just the same! If only there were a light *somewhere* so that you could get even a rough idea of just where you were in relation to the village! Eventually you figure out where you've gone wrong, and end up scrabbling through fences and melon fields to get back to the path you really should be on!

We are to shine God's word onto the paths of life that people are walking on. Sometimes they're on roads that are dead ends, but they don't realise it. Perhaps they think their good works will 'see them all right' in the end. But God's word has already shone a light onto that path to show us it will get us nowhere.

Other people have all sorts of ideas of what gives

life meaning and purpose. Many think they have to 'make their mark' at something – working their way up their career, getting the next car up in the range, being seen with the 'right' people. An interview with Marlon Brando recently showed up the emptiness and futility of this path:

> 'Despite intimations of a comeback, Brando's life remains shapeless. He said recently: "I don't like people; I don't love my neighbour. Every time I put any faith in love or friendship, I only came through with deep wounds. Today I am truly a person not open to relationships; this isn't a lie but a very true fact. I am deeply lonely, alone. I enjoy life, up to a point, but I no longer have dreams. Death and old age are events which I accept and await with all feasible serenity. To a certain extent at times I make of them the purpose of living: I work toward the point at which I can accept them with equanimity." '
>
> *Sunday Mirror Magazine, January 1989*

There must be more point to life than this! How are people to know that they were created for fellowship with God, and for exciting, creative stewardship of the earth, unless we tell them and help them to find their way back onto that path?

Go with them on the way

If there's a power cut we immediately search for the candles – and rack our brains to remember where we put them after the last power cut! It would be pretty useless to light a candle, stick it in a holder on the living room table, and expect it to give light all round the house. If we want to go into the kitchen or upstairs, we have to take the light with us.

In the same way, you and I are called to walk alongside people as guiding lights, helping them to see their way because of the way we are living, allowing them to copy the example we are giving. We lead the way by modelling it.

Bring the future into the present

We also lead the way in another sense. The God who has called us to serve him is the God who holds the future in his hands. As his servants, we are called to be 'makers of the future' with him. Gerald Coates calls it 'raiding the future for God'. With the insight God gives us, the power of prayer and with courage and determination, we are called to bring as much as we can of the kingdom of God – his future reign – into the present. Our brief is to change society in order to bring it into line with God's plans for it.

Light warns

Light is often used as a warning, perhaps over a hole in the road to show us where it is, so that we don't fall in. We are called to be warning lights in a society that is full of holes people are always falling into. We are to be like lights warning people away from styles of life, habits and attitudes that will corrupt them and destroy others.

A captain of an aircraft carrier was sailing up the channel, his lights all ablaze. In the distance he saw another bright point of light so, as he drew nearer, he sent out a message: 'Move two degrees to starboard.' The message came back, '*You* move two degrees to starboard.' Annoyed, the captain responded, '*You* move two degrees to starboard; I am a captain!' And the reply came back, '*You* move two degrees to starboard; I am an able seaman!' Infuriated, the captain sent back the command, 'Move two degrees to starboard; I am the captain of an aircraft carrier!' And the reply came back, 'You had *better* move two degrees to starboard; I am an able seaman in a lighthouse!'

Lighthouses are found in dangerous and lonely places. They get battered by storms in the course of their work, yet if they didn't stick it out many ships would be wrecked. Part of our calling to be the light of the world is to act as lighthouses in our society. That means we can't always stay comfortably on the shore, but may be called to go out to the black spots of life, where danger, unhappiness, violence and despair are at their worst. Many Christians are helping to care for the residents of 'Cardboard City' at Waterloo, in London. Some work on the city streets among prostitutes and drug addicts, bringing them the love of God. Some have established drug rehabilitation centres, like Yeldall Manor, and give their lives to working with potentially manipulative and violent people.

As a last point, remember that the light we are to shine into our world is not our own. That would never be strong enough to challenge the world nor to withstand the advance of darkness. To show others the light, we have to keep walking in the company of the Light himself, allowing him to shine into the dark corners of our own lives, sending the cockroaches running.

4

PLAYING BY THE RULES

I've seen some tremendous cricketers play. Some of them are 'naturals': with very little practice and effort they are simply brilliant! Of course, they *do* practise, but their performances *look* effortless. Others practise for hours at the kinds of stroke they need and they do OK at the match. They do all the right things, keep the rules of the game and produce a very workmanlike job. But it feels a bit of a plod. They don't have the sparkle of the genius who seems to live on a plane above the rules, creating a game that is a work of art.

Their gift seems to transcend the letter of the rule book. They are playing according to its spirit, rather than its technicalities.

It's the same with music. I am capable of playing every song in *Songs of Fellowship*, and I'd be really happy to lead worship on Sunday morning at church. But you would need to give me a year's notice for each song so that I could practise it! Eventually I'd be able to play them – and it would be a workmanlike job. But it would have nothing of the freedom and vitality that our 'real' musicians could give them. They play with an ease that betrays a gift; they do not have a commitment just to getting the notes, timing and rhythm right, but they are gifted by God with the ability to make it live.

When Jesus was baptised, God announced: 'You are my Son, whom I love; with you I am well pleased.' (Luke 3:22.) The appearance of the Spirit, like a dove above him at his baptism, confirmed that Jesus' life was totally, one hundred percent, pleasing to God. He wasn't just a 'plodder' who took care to keep every last little detail of the Law. Rather, because of his anointing with the Spirit, he was supernaturally endowed by God to live out the implications of the Law. That marked him out as someone very different and put him in conflict with the Pharisees – the best 'law keepers' of the day.

In Jesus' time 'the Law' sometimes meant just the ten commandments, sometimes the first five books of the Bible, sometimes all the Old Testament teaching and sometimes, and it's in this last way that the Pharisees and Scribes saw it, a vast collection of rules and regulations that had been written to explain exactly what the ten commandments meant.

For example, one of the ten commandments says, 'Remember the Sabbath day by keeping it holy . . . on it you shall not do any work' (Exodus 20:8, 10). The Pharisees had become terribly nit-picking about that and had tried to define it. What does it mean to 'work'? Well, it means you mustn't carry a burden. Well, how heavy is a burden? There was a debate raging among the Pharisees at the time of Jesus about whether a tailor was working on the Sabbath if he inadvertently went out with a pin in his coat! Things had got to that level of legalism and stupidity.

When the Pharisees spoke of the Law they meant

the whole thing, including all that they had added to it. When Jesus spoke of the Law he spoke of its heart – the ten commandments, and the meaning behind the words.

Jesus said:

> 'Do not think that I have come to abolish the Law or the Prophets; I have not come to abolish them but to fulfil them. I tell you the truth, until heaven and earth disappear, not the smallest letter, not the least stroke of a pen, will by any means disappear from the Law until everything is accomplished. Anyone who breaks one of the least of these commandments and teaches others to do the same will be called least in the kingdom of heaven, but whoever practises and teaches these commandments will be called great in the kingdom of heaven. For I tell you that unless your righteousness surpasses that of the Pharisees and the teachers of the law, you will certainly not enter the kingdom of heaven.'
>
> *Matthew 5: 17–20*

In other words, Jesus was saying he had not come to make the ten commandments redundant, but to live out their teachings perfectly. He didn't do so in a legalistic way, saying to himself, 'I must obey this rule, and I must not do that.' Rather, his life was so filled with God that he obeyed the Law supernaturally. The ten commandments are a written expression of what God is like, what he values and what he hates. God was so present in Jesus that the commandments were fulfilled naturally, almost automatically, by him. He was gifted by God with the Holy Spirit, who enabled him to do so.

TWO PITS

Jesus' fulfilling of the Law has massive implications for us. The fact that he kept it underlines that it is permanent. He said as much: 'until heaven and earth disappear, not the smallest letter, not the least stroke of a pen, will by any means disappear from the Law until everything is accomplished.' This tells us two things:-

- We must ourselves, as Jesus' disciples, keep the Old Testament Law of God, the ten commandments.
- But we do so not because we *must*, but because we are *empowered* to do so, by the same Holy Spirit who empowered Jesus. When we are filled with the Holy Spirit the Law really can work its truth out in our lives.

If either of these two things is separated from the other, we will end up with either legalism or licence.

Legalism

Many Christians are 'dry as dust' Christians. Perhaps they grew up in a traditional Christian home, they're nice people, they're clear about the need to obey God's Law – and they do so. But there's no life in it, no anointing of the Holy Spirit in their lives. We can keep the Law thoroughly in every tiny detail – even be the sort of Christians who won't used dried milk because the Bible says, 'Marvel not'! Our lives can be bound up with rules and regulations – mostly self-imposed ones like the Pharisees' – because we're afraid of stepping out of line and doing the wrong thing. Sometimes we can end up with a modern equivalent of the Pharisees' list of commandments: 'You shall not do the washing on Sunday. You shall not go to a pub. You shall not swear when you feel angry. You shall not spend lots of money on a holiday . . .' And if we break one of these self-made rules, we feel as guilty as if we had committed murder.

Licence

On the other hand, many people down through history, and some in recent years too, have said that the Law is dead and finished because we live in the age of the Spirit. They believe that because we have God's Spirit *in* us, we no longer need to bother with *external* law-keeping. Rules and regulations don't have any hold on us any more, we're free. We can forget the ten commandments.

But that is not the view of the New Testament. Yes, we *are* free, and we can be filled with the Holy Spirit, but this is so that we are *able* to fulfil the Law, not so that we can discard it. It is the Holy Spirit who takes it up and applies it in our lives, just as the gift of a musician enables her to use her technical skills to produce a real work of art.

Some of us are filled with the Spirit and our lives are full of vital signs of God at work. But is there also a moral maturity in our lives? The things we say and do should reveal a character in whom the fruit of the Spirit is at work. The standards and objective teaching of the Old and New Testaments should be evident in our lives.

Our salvation does not depend on our keeping the Law, but our desire to do so will flow naturally from our desire to please the God who has saved us. So we might not worry about doing the washing on Sunday, but we *will* look for positive ways to make not just

Sunday but every day 'holy' to God. We may have the freedom to enjoy a pint in the pub, but we will be aware that it is not always helpful to do so – alcoholism is a big problem today, even among some Christians. Our first desire will be to honour God in the way we live and the example we set for others, not to exercise our new freedom in Christ at any cost. It's the same with swearing and holidays. Freedom in Christ does not mean we can throw off all restraint. Rather, Jesus urges us to turn our minds to the positive, to look for the good things we can say and do that will build others up.

We cannot, then, sit loose to the great moral commands of the Old Testament. To do so would be to cut off Christianity from its roots. That would soon make our faith grow weak and wither. A rootless, subjective Christianity, based on a vague feeling of spirituality alone, is a useless Christianity. Our faith must have both an objective basis in the word of God, and the subjective anointing of the Holy Spirit.

The ten commandments are like channels down which the water of the Spirit flows. Without the Spirit they're just dry ruts. But our life in the Spirit will only be fulfilled when we are living in obedience to God as already defined by him in those commandments.

STEERING CLEAR OF THE PITS

How do we make sure we don't fall into the pit of legalism or the pit of licence?

Ask for a change of will

Paul wrote, 'Where the Spirit of the Lord is, there is freedom' (2 Corinthians 3:17). Liberty, or freedom, is not the same as licence. We are not free to do as we please, but neither are we to allow ourselves to get locked into obedience from a sense of duty. Our freedom is the freedom to be filled with the Holy Spirit so that by his power our will is changed. If we *want* to do the right thing, doing it is not so much hassle!

You might be very attracted to someone of the opposite sex who is not your wife or husband. It is virtually impossible *not* to want to take things further, unless that would mean throwing away something you want more badly. Perhaps you want more than anything else to cultivate a good relationship with your spouse. Or it might be that you want above all to honour Jesus in the way you live. And because those desires are greater than the desire to give in to temptation, you end up doing the right thing.

Duty and love are intermingled in our obedience to God. Our wills are *informed* by the ten commandments, but *motivated* by love for God.

It's the difference between doing something because the headmaster tells you to, and doing something because your father asks you to. A child will obey the headmaster out of fear of what might happen if he doesn't. But he'll obey his father out of love and trust, and because he wants to please him. Once we know we are forgiven and accepted by our heavenly Father, we no longer keep his laws out of fear of reprisals – we know he's not like that; we keep them out of love for him.

Or take marriage. If I say to Jan I'm going to be back by a certain time in the evening, I usually make sure I am; not because I'm afraid of what Jan might do if I'm late, but because I love her and don't want her to be worried.

Depend on God's grace

It is important to understand what we *cannot* achieve by keeping the Law. Jesus must have sent shock waves through the crowd when he said, 'Those leaders you've got – the Scribes and Pharisees – look at how righteous they are! They keep every minute detail of the law. But if you want to get into the kingdom of heaven, you will have to be even more spiritual and righteous than they are!'

Why did Jesus say that? Because keeping the Law will not save us. We do not earn salvation; we are given it as a free gift when we put our faith in the righteousness of Jesus.

Many people today believe they will be accepted by God on the basis of their works. Almost anyone who doesn't really know the heart of the gospel message will say to you and me, 'Well, I go to church; I try to be kind and neighbourly; I do my best – and you can't ask more than that, can you?' What they're saying is that obedience to some law, their own set of ideals and values, will make them acceptable to God. And that was the Pharisees in a nutshell. 'If we obey all the laws in the Old Testament, and throw in several thousand of our own too, then we'll be acceptable to God.'

But Jesus cuts a knife right through that way of thinking: 'You can obey every single law, and a thousand more you haven't even thought of yet, but you'll never get into the kingdom of God – because that's not the way to get in. The only way is through faith in me.'

Many people are trying hard to 'win God over' to their side, by doing a lot of good things. Perhaps you are one of them. Although you became a Christian by faith, perhaps you now feel you need to live it by works. It's as if there's a list of things in heaven that we can get Brownie points for; a sort of house points system. If we're nice enough and good enough, often enough, God will bless us and our crown will be bigger!

Have you noticed, for example, that new Christians often catch a disease called 'Meetingitis'? We can feel we need to prove ourselves worthy of being saved, or we want to express our gratitude to God in a visible way – hence Meetingitis: an unfortunate compulsion to attend every house group, prayer meeting or Sunday service possible! It isn't necessary. We *stay* saved, just as we *got* saved, by God's grace, not by our good works. For new Christians with husbands and wives who do not yet share their faith, it can in fact be far more important to stay at home with them! Many non-Christian husbands feel they've lost their wives to 'God' when their wives become Christians. If such wives are not careful about the number of meetings they go to, their husbands can become very resentful of having lost them to 'the church' too.

AN EXAMPLE

Jesus wanted to make sure the people really understood what he was saying about keeping God's rules, and about the need to go further than *simply* keeping the rules. So he went on to give them an example:

> 'You have heard that it was said to the people long ago, "Do not murder, and anyone who murders will be subject to judgment." But I tell you that anyone who is angry with his brother will be subject to judgment. Again, anyone who says to his brother, "Raca," is answerable to the Sanhedrin. But anyone who says, "You fool!" will be in danger of the fire of hell.'
>
> *Matthew 5:21–22*

Murder dissected

If you dissect murder, taking it apart bit by bit, you will find particular attitudes, opinions and values at its heart. All of these desperately need to be dealt with long before they develop into actual murder.

It seems that Jesus had in mind three 'stages' in the development of murder:

Smouldering resentment

'Anyone who is angry with his brother will be subject to judgment,' said Jesus. The word Jesus uses for 'angry' means 'to go on being angry'. It's the sort of situation where you have been wronged and hurt. Perhaps someone at work has hurt you by what they've said or how they've treated you. Perhaps it's your husband, wife or parents. 'How could they say such a thing?' you ask yourself. 'I was doing my best; couldn't they see that?'

We can be wounded easily – and deeply – by our marriage partners. Sometimes the hurt and resentment can go on festering for years because we've never come to terms with it. We haven't forgiven them. Superficially your relationship may look great but deep inside resentment continues to smoulder.

The Lord wants us to be free from this because, if we allow it to carry on unchecked, it will eat away into our souls, as deadly and destructive as any physical cancer. It will poison our relationship with our partner, damage our relationship with God because we are not being totally honest with him, and make our worship and witness shallow.

Sooner or later, the smouldering volcano erupts. We may strike out at someone, or perhaps a family relationship is blown apart. Sometimes we're so good at containing the way we feel that the emotional pain surfaces in the form of physical illness.

This resentment, allowed to burn unchecked, says Jesus, lies at the heart of the act of murder. And the commandment, 'You shall not murder', given so long ago in the Old Testament, means first, 'You shall not allow resentment to smoulder away inside you. Deal with it!' We deal with it by taking it honestly to God, confessing it to him, and asking for his forgiveness. Forgiveness doesn't mean pretending something bad didn't happen after all, but it cleanses the wounds so that we can be healed of its effects. Forgiveness doesn't mean allowing things to go on as before, but it enables us to go on loving, and to repair relationships. God longs to give us his healing for those wounds, deep in our beings. By opening the door of forgiveness we open the door of our lives again to the person who has wronged us, and we open the door to Jesus too, so that he can come in to heal and restore.

Contemptuous dismissal

'Again, anyone who says to his brother, "Raca," is answerable to the Sanhedrin.' This is the next stage that Jesus points to. If you've read this passage before, I expect you've wondered what on earth 'Raca' means. Is it short for racoon?! What is a raca? Well, the reason why it has not been translated from the Aramaic is that it is impossible to convey its meaning in just one or two words. I suppose the nearest equivalent might be something like 'brainless idiot!'

The attitude betrayed by such a derogatory insult is one of contemptuous dismissal. The person doing the insulting denies the other person's ability to think or reason. It's exactly what happens if we allow our anger and resentment towards someone to go unchecked. We begin to be contemptuous of them and everything about them – their thinking, their gifts, abilities and the things they do. We are always criticising and finding fault. We dismiss their ideas without a second thought. They could suggest something really good, or at least perfectly sensible, but because we've already shut ourselves off from them we instantly dismiss their suggestions. It's the smoke from that smouldering resentment, blinding our eyes to all that is good in them and clouding our judgment so that we are unable to make wise and godly decisions about them.

Jesus calls us to take a fresh look at ourselves. OK, so we might not have murdered, but is our attitude one that lies at the heart of murder? We might not have run someone down in our car, but are we running them down by what we say – belittling their mind, gifts and all that they do? What is it that we're holding against them, resenting about them? We must search our own hearts and dig out every last little bit of it.

Degrading the person

'Anyone who says, "You fool!" will be in danger of the fire of hell.' This is Jesus' description of the third stage on the road to murder.

It is not much easier to translate the word for 'fool' than it is to translate 'raca'! It doesn't mean just ignorant, unwise or unthinking; rather, it denotes a moral stupidity. It is a criticism of someone's total personhood. He's a total 'waste of space'; 'good for nothing'; of absolutely no value whatever. In biblical language, a 'fool' is someone who has no moral sense at all. He has become incapable of doing anything good.

If we think this about someone we are in severe danger of treating him as an 'it'. And that is the ultimate blasphemy – to look at someone for whom Christ died and to dismiss that person as worthless. Once we think of someone as less than human it is a short step to abusing them and even to feeling there is nothing wrong with their murder. Religious people are often the worst culprits here. Think of Saul of Tarsus. He was so contemptuous of the bunch of oddballs who said that a man, Jesus, was God, that he regarded them as less than human – a disgrace to good Jewish society – so not fit to live. And so he did all he could to destroy them (see Acts 7:54–8:3; 9:1–2; 26:4–11). Jesus, however, reminds us that because all people are made in the image of God, all people have unique dignity and value.

COMING INTO LINE WITH THE RULES

So, we have to get rid of our resentments and bitterness in order for God's Spirit to be able to work effectively in us and help us live according to the Law of God. That's all very well, but how?

Be honest with God

If we allow ourselves to be controlled by our feelings, we will find that our relationship with God is stunted, just as much as our relationships with other people are:

> 'Therefore, if you are offering your gift at the altar and there remember that your brother has something against you, leave your gift there in front of the altar. First go and be reconciled to your brother; then come and offer your gift.
>
> Settle matters quickly with your adversary who is taking you to court. Do it while you are still with him on the way, or he may hand you over to the judge, and the judge may hand you over to the officer, and you may be thrown into prison. I tell you the truth, you will not get out until you have paid the last penny.' *Matthew 5:23–26*

Bad relationships can hinder worship. Superficially, our relationship with Jesus may seem all right, but deep inside we struggle to be released into worship and praise. It's as if we've covered our spirits with a veneer of resentment, and it prevents God breaking through to us in the way he wants to. And often we're hindered even from coming into the presence of God because of our anger and frustration about other people.

Bad relationships hinder our corporate worship

too. If a congregation is divided and hurting from broken relationships and bitterness towards one another, the body of Christ is fragmented and cannot offer him true worship.

The whole purpose of Jesus' death on the cross was to reconcile us to God, and ourselves to each other. When you get your bank statement, you probably go through your cheque book stubs to see what *you* think the balance of your account should be. And then you check with the bank statement again and wonder why it says something completely different! So you try to reconcile the two, seeing if the bank has lost a cheque, or hasn't acted on a request to cancel a standing order, or if something else has happened. You try to bring the two accounts into line so that they balance and match. Reconciliation is what we need to work for, too, in our corporate life as God's people. It's not that we need always to think the same or do the same things, but by becoming reconciled to God we have entered into an agreement with him to love and be reconciled to one another, too. If our *worship* of God for what he has done for us is to have any meaning, we need to be *acting* on what he has done for us – being reconciled to one another.

As we allow God to deal with us in this way, we will discover new freedom and release in our worship, both individually and corporately.

Be prepared to forgo your 'rights'

Jesus calls us to a maturity that is prepared to forgo our 'rights'. When I'm really hurt or angry about something that has been done or said unjustly about me, I find it helpful to remember that my suffering is nothing compared to the unjust hurt Jesus suffered on my behalf. Sometimes when we're criticised unjustly we can get all upset and stay in a crotchety, bad-tempered mood for months! If it weren't so sad, our over-reactions would really be quite funny. It's strange that when we get *praise* which we don't deserve, we don't seem to mind that at all! Nor do we plunge into the same terrible moods!

Sometimes people say to me, 'I've got a right to be angry about this.' 'Yes,' I'll agree, 'you have. But it's still not right!' We need to learn to sit more loosely to our 'right' to be judged for who we really are. It's probably a good thing people don't actually know what we're really like! Jesus calls us to forgo our 'rights' and to exercise instead our privilege as members of the kingdom of God – the privilege to forgive, to know his healing from smouldering resentment, and from the contemptuous dismissal of others.

Change the way you behave

We cannot easily change how we feel about someone, but we can make up our mind to behave towards them in a loving, gracious and kind way, despite our feelings. If I've fallen out with my brother or sister in Christ I must *do* something to change that situation: I must 'go and be reconciled'. It's no use carrying on as usual, coming to worship, offering ourselves and our gifts to God, and hoping we might just feel different afterwards.

Resentment is expressed as a feeling, but it isn't just a feeling; it is an action. It works its way out in actions. If I resent someone, I'll go out of my way to snub him and do him down. The answer is not to wait until my feelings change, but to act now *as if I did not feel any resentment to him at all.* So, although I may still feel hurt by a particular person, I'll go out of my way to encourage him, vote for him, take him a birthday cake – whatever I can to promote his good and well-being. If we *do* what we know is right, we will soon *feel* like doing what is right. Feelings follow actions.

In his book, *Mere Christianity*, C S Lewis points out that we are to become in practice what we already are in theory – sons and daughters of God who live like Christ. He writes:

> 'When you are not feeling particularly friendly but know you ought to be, the best thing you can do, very often, is to put on a friendly manner and behave as if you were a nicer person than you actually are. And in a few minutes, as we have all noticed, you will be really feeling friendlier than you were. Very often the only way to get a quality in reality is to start behaving as if you had it already . . .
>
> Now, the moment you realise, "Here I am, dressing up as Christ," it is extremely likely that you will see at once some way in which at that very moment the pretence could be made less of a pretence and more of a reality. You will find several things going on in your mind which would not be going on there if you were really a son of God. Well, stop them. Or you may realise that, instead of saying your prayers, you ought to be downstairs writing a letter, or helping your wife to wash up. Well, go and do it . . . The real Son of God is at your side. He is beginning to turn you into the same kind of thing as himself.' *C S Lewis, 'Mere Christianity'. London: Fontana, 1970.*

5

PURE IN HEART

The *Daily Mirror* ran an article in its 29 May 1991 issue, titled, 'Adultery . . . the sin that dreams are made of.' It went on to say:

'Women are catching up fast in the sex war – but can men cope with this kind of equality? There's worrying news for them in a revealing *Daily Mirror* poll which paints a startling picture of Britain in the Nineties.

'It seems it's just as acceptable these days for HER to enjoy steamy fantasies about the man next door or imagine herself in a torrid clinch with a screen hero as it is for HIM to drool over a pin-up.

'But here's worse news: she night actually pop next door to try the real thing. For one woman in four, according to our amazing survey, now thinks that adultery is OK.'

Adultery and divorce have affected society for many years. But in a society like ours in which divorce is an increasingly more popular way of dealing with problems within marriage, and when the sexual side of our lives is more open and more freely discussed, Jesus' words to us hit home like sledgehammer blows. What he expects from his disciples in terms of sexual purity is in stark contrast to what we see around us today:

> 'You have heard that it was said, "Do not commit adultery." But I tell you that anyone who looks at a woman lustfully has already committed adultery with her in his heart. If your right eye causes you to sin, gouge it out and throw it away. It is better for you to lose one part of your body than for your whole body to be thrown into hell. And if your right hand causes you to sin, cut it off and throw it away. It is better for you to lose one part of your body than for your whole body to go into hell.'
>
> *Matthew 5:27–30*

KEEPING SEXUALLY PURE

No Christian writes out of perfection when he writes on the area of sexual sin. In becoming Christians we don't lose our humanity, nor our capacity to be tempted. What does Jesus tell us about this area of our lives?

Control your thought life

In the last chapter we saw that it is our thought life that produces anger and hatred, the root causes of murder. Murders don't just 'happen'. Here again, Jesus gets to the heart of the problem of adultery. He leaves no room for the snooty and arrogant to say, 'Well, of course, that's not *my* problem – that's something other people do.' Tragically, many Christians are involved in adultery and many have suffered divorce.

Jesus shows that adultery is not simply a matter of

expressing sexuality outside the marriage bond. It's more a matter of the thought in your mind, dwelt on, entertained, encouraged – *even though no action occurs as a result*! That, Jesus says, is what is at the heart of adultery. The challenge to all of us, then, whether we're married or single, is to exercise holiness and purity about our thought life. God is concerned that our whole being should reflect his own holiness. King David put it this way, 'You desire truth in the inner parts' – in our thoughts and desires, not just in our actions; 'you teach me wisdom in the inmost place' (Psalm 51:6). It is that inner purity which we need to cultivate, with God's help.

What kind of pictures are we letting our minds feed on? They need to be rigorously monitored. If you watch a lot of television or see adverts in the press or on hoardings, you can't possibly be in any doubt that our sexual desires are being exploited for commercial purposes. In the advertising industry, sex is used to sell everything from cars to cat food! Quite unjustifiably and illegitimately, we are being conned into believing that sex and sexuality are the yardstick by which the value of everything in life can be measured.

As a result, hardly anyone can have failed to get the message: 'Have you noticed that all the best people are sexually attractive? You want to be one of the best people in your town? You buy this fantastic product and you'll be an instant hit! Just you see if you don't get all the admiration and respect you deserve! Be wise! Get on in the world! Buy X!' The pressure is on to *prove* that we're sexually attractive. What better proof than having an affair?

This invasion of our minds is persistent and subtle.

We hardly notice that our attitudes and expectations have changed.

This doesn't happen just to non-Christians! Of the people I trained with for the Baptist ministry, six of them had left the ministry before they'd been in it seven years, because of adultery. In one eighteen-month period a major denomination removed twelve ministers from office, because of their adultery. Of the first fifty people to die of AIDS in this country, two were Anglican clergymen. I am saddened to hear almost weekly of Christian leaders I have known and cared for personally, or known by reputation, whose marriages are in a mess. They are broken, hurt, defeated men and women, trying to put their lives back together again.

And those are just the leaders! We all seem to have swallowed the world's poisonous message that free sexual expression is a legitimate 'bit of fun' – in fact, it is our 'right', and crucial to our emotional and psychological well-being! It's not given a second thought. So now, even to most Christians, the church's traditional teaching of 'chastity outside marriage and faithfulness inside marriage' sounds embarrassingly old-fashioned. The word 'chaste' is seen as something dredged up from the dark ages of repression, and words like 'liberated', 'freedom', 'self-expression' and 'self-fulfilment' have become the new religious catch-words.

It is, in fact, something of a new religion. And in a society which follows that religion slavishly, Jesus calls his followers to be the heretics.

How do we measure up to his expectations of us? Which of us men has not seen an attractive woman on television or walking down the street, or even in church, and not let our minds do things which they ought not to have done, and then dwelt on it and encouraged those thoughts? If you allow your thought life to wander, beware! I am convinced that the only reason there isn't more sin in this area among Christians is not that we're spiritual enough to resist it, but simply that we don't have the opportunity. If we did, many of us would find that our thoughts were quickly leading us on into action.

Be aware of your weak points

God is not calling us to be paranoid! Neither should our concern to be pure, sexually, lead us to see sex as something unclean. It sounds as easy as walking a tightrope blindfolded! Well, here are some of the problem areas we'll be hitting sooner or later, and some steps to take to overcome them.

The need for friendship and affirmation

We need friends to share life with; we often need affirmation. But how do we try to meet these needs? It's flattering to have someone of the opposite sex take an interest in you and want to spend time with you. But it's easy to take advantage of that friendship and use it simply to bolster your own ego. It's hard to be honest with ourselves about our motives, which is why it's doubly important to be transparently honest with God, bringing all our friendships, all our words, thoughts and actions into the powerful light of his gaze. Charles Finney said, 'Keep short accounts with God'. And John Donne strongly advised going over those accounts with God at the end of each day: 'Sleep with clean hands, either kept clean all day by integrity or washed clean at night by repentance.'

A marriage under pressure

All marriages go through rocky patches – perhaps the husband is under a lot of pressure at work, so time together is short. And when they are together, he's so preoccupied with work that he's deadly boring! Perhaps finances are strained and the pleasure of going out somewhere together is spoiled because you're wondering what you're going to have to go without as a result. Perhaps the children are being a real pain and each partner ends up ratty and blaming the other for not controlling them better. The devil is always looking for chinks in marriages, especially Christian ones, that he can exploit, widening the divisions between husband and wife. Keep your eyes open to what's happening in your marriage – no one but the devil wins the battles between you and your spouse!

Gerald Griffin has said, 'Society creates the myth that marriage is the proper haven for all our longings and a cure for all our shortcomings. People are programmed to believe that marriage will automatically give them individuality, identity, security, and happiness, when as a matter of fact marriage gives them none of these things unless they possess them in the first place.' Trouble can start when either marriage partner realises that the other simply cannot meet all their human and spiritual needs, so assumes that their partner is failing. That's the time when many people feel justified in looking to someone other than their husband or wife for the fulfilment they think they should be getting. Of course, it's vital that we have close friends outside our marriages – but a substitute husband or wife is another matter altogether. It's important that we find our ultimate confidence in Jesus, not our marriage partner. It's Jesus who gives us dignity and respect. It's his honour and reputation we live for. And that will radically affect the way we relate to our marriage partner. It will mean that, even if they are short-changing us in some way, we'll be able to go on loving and caring for them, for Jesus' sake.

Opportunity
Perhaps you work closely with someone of the opposite sex. Perhaps people come to you to talk about their problems and you find yourself drawn very close to someone in particular. Perhaps you are just sociable and enjoy other people's company.

It is vital to give ourselves some basic 'ground rules' that we will always stick to in these situations. What those are will vary to some extent for each of us because we each have different areas of weakness. In his book, *Hedges*, Jerry Jenkins lists six 'hedges' or rules he's given himself in order to protect his marriage: First, if he needs to meet, travel or eat out with another woman, he'll always make it a threesome. He believes it's important that his actions could not be misinterpreted by anyone looking on. Second, he's careful how he touches people, and will embrace others only in public. Third, he's careful about how he compliments other women. Fourth, flirting is out, full stop. Fifth, he makes sure his wife knows his ground rules, and that he keeps to them! Sixth, he sets a curfew on work. He leaves it behind at a certain time, and refuses to let it encroach on time that belongs to his wife and family. (See *Hedges*: *Loving Your Marriage Enough to Protect it*, Jerry Jenkins. Brentwood, USA: Wolgemuth & Hyatt.)

Discouragement
This can hit us at any time – and it usually seems to come when we're already down and depressed! Instead of looking for a quick 'fix' in the supportive friendship of someone else, channel your time and energies back into your family. Other projects we work on come and go. We can put a whole year's work into something only to find it all collapse. God has entrusted us with our families for the whole of our lifetimes, so it is never a waste of time or energy to give ourselves wholeheartedly to them.

A false sense of security
The people I fear for most are those who think they will never succumb to sexual sin. A healthy scepticism of our own ability to resist temptation is a surer safeguard. 'God have mercy on me, a sinner,' is a wiser attitude than, 'Look at me! I fast twice a week – aren't I good?' We're all fallible. Let's not forget that nor belittle the strength of the opposition. We're never strong enough to risk walking into temptation.

Many of these factors recur again and again. And so will the temptations that go with them. O A Battista has said, 'Temptations, unlike opportunities, will always give you a second chance.' The battle is one that has to be fought and won time and again as we struggle to fix our eyes on Jesus.

DIVORCE

> 'It has been said, "Anyone who divorces his wife must give her a certificate of divorce." But I tell you

> that anyone who divorces his wife, except for marital unfaithfulness, causes her to become an adulteress, and anyone who marries the divorced woman commits adultery.'
>
> *Matthew 5:31–32*

Jesus again cuts to the heart of this issue and says that divorce isn't something you just do, one day; it's built up over a number of years. Bad attitudes that go unconfessed and unforgiven, resentments that build up and increasing hardness of heart are what eventually lead to divorce. Divorce doesn't come suddenly out of a loving relationship; it's built up over months and years of unresolved conflict, pain and tension. And sometimes one partner can be completely unaware that these things are building up in the other.

God's view

In Malachi, God states clearly, 'I hate divorce' (Malachi 2:16). He binds two people together as one flesh in marriage and when that's ripped apart he hates it. He hates the pain, the crying of the children feeling confused, guilty, frightened and bereft of a parent. He hates the desperate pain of the wronged partners who cry themselves to sleep at night unable to find relief from their hurt and powerlessness. That's why God hates it, because he sees his creation smashed beyond recognition; hurt, damaged and bent out of shape. God never thinks divorce is good, although sometimes it appears to be the better of two very bad options. Personally, I could never actively encourage anyone to get a divorce, although if they felt they had to, I as their pastor, along with the entire congregation, would want to pray for them, give them support and love, and not be judgemental.

The Old Testament could not have been clearer about God's view of marriage and divorce, but in Jesus' day Jewish men said that if you wanted to divorce your wife, you could. Just give her a certificate to confirm it! It was fairly easy, really – if she put too much salt in your food, or you saw someone who looked a bit better, you could just divorce her.

Of course, that was a gross travesty of what God had intended for marriage and Jesus reaffirmed that divorce is always wrong – except in the case of 'marital unfaithfulness'. Exactly what he meant by this is not as clear as it might seem. The Greek word used is *porneia*, from which we derive our word pornography and the associated idea of sexual abuse. The way the NIV translates it – 'marital unfaithfulness' – implies sexual unchastity, though Jesus might have meant unfaithfulness more broadly. Perhaps, for instance, the wife is undergoing persistent physical violence; her husband is thereby denying their marriage relationship and being unfaithful to it. Perhaps she is subjected to a different sort of 'marital unfaithfulness'.

Whatever it was Jesus had in mind, it was certainly something severe and destructive. He wasn't thinking of the trivial, 'we just don't seem to love each other any more,' reason for divorce. It's actually not until that point has been reached, when the *feeling* of love goes, that *real* love starts! Love is a commitment of the will. In my view, there are very few occasions which genuinely justify divorce, and those are mostly to do with the sexual immorality of one partner.

God longs to restore

If you have been divorced, know that Jesus doesn't write you off in any way, shape or form. He hates divorce, but he loves people who have been divorced, because he loves people. Divorce is not the ultimate sin. God can forgive you of all that led up to that, just as he can forgive you of any sinful thinking or behaviour. Perhaps you're living in the pain of a broken relationship, perhaps you're in the middle of divorce proceedings. Or perhaps the agony of a past divorce, maybe from many years ago, is still with you. Know that God, too, is with you in that. He feels the pain with you, and he longs to build you up again from it. He wants to bring you to a point of repentance and faith where the past can be put behind you and the sins and mistakes that led to that marriage breakdown are forgiven and resolved by his power.

God is not a God only of the past, he's a God who can take the mistakes of the past, help us face them square on, and bring blessings out of them for the future. Joel brings us God's promise: 'I will restore to you the years the locusts have eaten' (Joel 2:25). He wants us to have a renewed, guilt-free relationship with him. He can take and deal with all the years of pain and twistedness that we've lived through, and wants to assure us of his love. If you've been through divorce, you will know that much of the pain comes through being avoided by your neighbours, criticised by your friends, and having previously mutual friends take sides over who is to blame. God's love for us is constant. He sees all that is worst in us, and loves us anyway. He looks at all that is good in us, and encourages that to develop. He never avoids us, rejects us, or writes us off.

Divorce, a heart attitude

Yet again, Jesus is not content to say, 'So, you've never been divorced . . . then this doesn't apply to you.' What about those of us who are married, and for whom divorce is something we've hardly considered – at least, not seriously? This week, we may have taken a step down that road without even realising it. The moment we hold onto a dark resentment, refusing to bring it out into the light of the open, or are hurt by our partner and won't admit to it or talk it through, then we have pushed our partner a little further away. It only seems one step, hardly any distance at all, but it's the beginning of the movement away. Divorce is not a piece of paper that says, 'you two are now separated.' It's a heart attitude that keeps a partner at arm's length.

Such heart separation may never end in the divorce courts, in physical separation. But in heart and mind we have divorced our partner; we can already be distancing ourselves from them in a way that God never intended. Jesus' word to us is, 'Deal with that now. Make sure your marriage relationship is right *today*.'

As husbands and wives we need to speak openly with each other about the sexual temptations we face, and to pray together about them. Single people need friends with whom they can share their struggles – friends who will be sensitive to their needs, pray with them, help and comfort them.

A 10,000 mile service

Every marriage needs regular servicing if it is to keep running smoothly. How can we do this?

- Several Christian organisations run 'marriage enrichment' weekends; it would be worth having a look at them and considering going on one.
- Ask some good friends, preferably a couple who have been married longer, to talk with you about your marriage. What does it look like to them? Do they see how things could be improved? Do they recognise any danger points? We need people who are close enough to know when things are going wrong, objective enough to help us sort out what we should do to put things right, and laid-back enough not to be embarrassed about it!
- From time to time, review what is happening in each of the four areas that cause most trouble in marriage: communication (lack of it), money, in-laws, and sex. As our circumstances change, so our relationship with each of these will too. Broadly, are things better in each area than they were, say, a year ago? Why? What has caused the changes for the better or the worse? How would you like things to be in this area of your marriage? What can you do to help work towards that?

6

A TRANSPARENT LIFE

When he was twenty-four years old, Abraham Lincoln served as the postmaster of New Salem, Illinois, for which he was paid an annual salary of $55.70. The New Salem post office was closed in 1836, but it was several years before the tax man arrived to settle accounts with ex-postmaster Lincoln, who was by then a lawyer, struggling to make a living and not doing too well. He was informed that $17 was due the government. Lincoln crossed the room, opened an old trunk and took out a yellowed cotton rag bound with string. Untying it, he spread out the cloth and there was the $17. He had kept it untouched for all those years. 'I never use any man's money but my own,' he said. No wonder his nickname was 'Honest Abe'!

NO HIDDEN MEANINGS

> 'Again, you have heard that it was said to the people long ago, "Do not break your oath, but keep the oaths you have made to the Lord." But I tell you, Do not swear at all: either by heaven, for it is God's

> throne; or by the earth, for it is his footstool; or by Jerusalem, for it is the city of the Great King. And do not swear by your head, for you cannot make even one hair white or black. Simply let your "Yes" be "Yes," and your "No," "No"; anything beyond this comes from the evil one.
>
> *Matthew 5:33–37*

Cross my heart and hope to die!

This passage is not really to do with our language, words that your parents would tell you off for saying. It's more to do with telling the truth: 'Let your "Yes" be "Yes," and your "No," "No." ' It was a custom in Jesus' day to swear by something in order to confirm a promise. You would swear by something enduring, or something whose continued existence was of major importance to you. So a devout Jew might swear by heaven, earth, Jerusalem, or even by his own bushy beard. What their swearing meant was, 'I promise you that my word will hold good for as long as the heavens/earth/Jerusalem itself stays intact.' Or, 'If I don't fulfil this promise to you, I will shave off this bushy beard of which I am so proud.' Sometimes they would swear 'by my strong right arm', meaning, 'If I don't do as I say I will, may my right arm and all its power wither away.'

We don't swear to a promise in this way today, but I have heard people say, 'Oh, I didn't feel I had to keep my word; after all, I hadn't promised.' Does this mean we can say what we like and not be bound by it as long as we don't put 'I promise . . .' in front of it?

As children, we used to have a game. We'd cross

our fingers and put our hands behind our backs and then whatever we said didn't count. So if Mum asked, 'Have you done your homework?' you could lie and say, 'Yes', provided you'd got your fingers crossed behind your back! I remember one occasion when I came unstuck with this. In our hallway was a huge mirror and I made the mistake of standing in front of it when Mum asked me about something. I lied, keeping my fingers crossed behind my back so that there wouldn't be any need to keep to what I'd said. But, of course, Mum saw exactly what I was doing. From then on, any important questions had to be answered with our hands held out in front of us! We could no longer worm our way out of doing something we didn't want to!

As adults, we go on playing children's games when it comes to transparent honesty. We'll sometimes do anything to get out of keeping an agreement, particularly if we've promised something rashly, in a hurry or under pressure. When we genuinely can't keep a promise, we ought to be up front about it and say so. Go to the person concerned and apologise. Instead, we often just hide. Quietly, we just don't do as we said we would. If we're ruthlessly honest about it, we often let one another down, often fail to deliver on something we promised we would: 'I'll let you know on Monday.' 'Don't worry – I'll run that errand for you.' Or the classic one, 'You can tell me; it won't go any further!' I've heard children in the playground saying, 'I won't tell anyone! Honest! Cross my heart and hope to die!' Well, that's our equivalent of the sort of oath undertaken in Jesus' day and, if God took us up on it, we'd all have been dead long since!

Say what you mean and mean what you say

Jesus points out that this sort of playing with words is an attempt to hide ourselves and our true intentions. It is an attempt to foil the other person. 'That's not the way you should carry on,' he says to his disciples. 'Simply say what you mean, and mean what you say.'

Much that happens in the church would be transformed by this simple principle! Life would be so much easier if we knew we could always rely on one another to do what we've said we would – or not do what we said we wouldn't. As someone has commented rather cynically, 'A secret is something you tell one person at a time!'

NO HIDDEN RESENTMENTS

Jesus' country was in the grip of an occupying power – the Romans. Their soldiers were everywhere. And they took advantage of their power. A Roman soldier, fed up with carrying his gear, could say to anyone passing on their way to the shops, 'Oi! Carry that stuff for me for the next mile.' And the unfortunate shopper would have to forget his trip and concentrate on the soldier's baggage. Someone commandeered in this way would feel resentful and totally humiliated. So the next words in Jesus' sermon would have jarred horribly on any Israelite ear – most of the situations here are probably descriptions of encounters with Roman soldiers:

> 'You have heard that it was said, "Eye for eye, and tooth for tooth." But I tell you, Do not resist an evil

> person. If someone strikes you on the right cheek, turn to him the other also. And if someone wants to sue you and take your tunic, let him have your cloak as well. If someone forces you to go one mile, go with him two miles. Give to the one who asks you and do not turn away from the one who wants to borrow from you.' *Matthew 5:38–42*

Revenge is usually our first, instinctive thought when we have been wronged and humiliated. For the Israelites under Roman occupation it was doubly galling to be abused and have no way of redress. They hated the Romans and wanted nothing to do with them. The thought of having to help one of them by carrying his bags (who knows what people he might be laying into when his hands were free?) was just sickening beyond words. You would feel like an accomplice; a forced traitor.

The 'strike' on the right cheek would have been a brutal blow from a soldier's right fist. In a way, it would have been a 'compassionate' bashing, as it meant he had decided not to go for you with his sword. But as he gripped his sword in his right hand, so he would knock you viciously out of his way with the butt of the sword or his right fist. A knock to the jaw like that could knock you out. It wasn't a gentle slap Jesus had seen – it was a fist in the face.

The quarrelsome person eager to sue another would demand the defendant's coat as surety against the claim. That would be humiliating enough, but Jesus tells his disciples to offer their cloaks too – their warm, outer garment – even though that was against the law on humanitarian grounds. Poor people used their cloaks as blankets at night (see Exodus 22:25–27).

The person who constantly wants to borrow things can be a real pain! It's often inconvenient to lend things; you don't know how they'll be treated or if you'll even get them back in one piece.

The principle Jesus lays down in each of these examples is: Always be ready to forgive. Don't hold resentments and grudges against people. Don't look for revenge or even a fair return – give freely. In Paul's words, 'Do not be overcome by evil; but overcome evil with good' (Romans 12:21).

Jesus' command to the disciple who's just had his dentures knocked out by a Roman soldier, is to forgive him. Instantly. So instantly, that he can turn the other cheek to him there and then. If someone hurts me a little, I can usually find it in me to forgive him. But when someone hurts me a great deal, it is very painful – not physically perhaps, but emotionally and mentally. What if they have done damage to my family? My career? My reputation? Jesus' teaching is clear and firm, 'Don't look for revenge.'

If someone offends us at work, makes us look stupid in front of the boss, or lies about us behind our back, we want to get back at them. As a child, if someone bullied me at school or got me into trouble with the teacher, I could always get some of my friends together, lie in wait for the culprit after school and duff him up on the way home. As adults we just duff them up in a more sophisticated fashion! We hope the person who's ruined our chances gets their own chances ruined. We hope their next bit of work is a failure. We exclude them from our conversations at coffee break and avoid them in the staff canteen. That's revenge – it just comes in a different guise.

If I'm resentful of things someone in the fellowship has said about me, it's very tempting to give a subtle 'slant' to my next sermon. That person will know exactly what I'm saying and why – and the feeling of getting my revenge would be sweet! But it is still revenge and I cannot hide it under the guise of 'relevant teaching'. Or I think, 'Perhaps I won't invite them round to our house after all.' But, according to Jesus, the principle I *should* be working on goes something like this: 'The nastier and ruder you are to me, the nicer I'll be to you and the more interesting things I'll invite you to!' In practice this means that if someone is derogatory about something I've written, I'll try to recommend something of his. If someone tears into something I've been trying to do, saying what a hopeless mess it is and what a stupid idea it all was in the first place anyway, I'll try to find some way of encouraging her in something she's doing.

Defensive action

When Saddam Hussein invaded Kuwait in August 1990, the western world was appalled and promptly set about counter attacking in order to get him out again. Does Jesus rule this out? What about self defence – should we simply let people pulverise us into the ground?

Many people have got their thinking tangled up here because they take Jesus' words to individual disciples and apply them to the national policies of world powers. Jesus wasn't addressing governments. Neither is he wiping out all differences between good and evil, justice and injustice. At both national and individual level it is right, wise and good to defend ourselves against those who attack us.

On a personal level, it is important to take defensive action against those who attack us, if at all possible, whether that attack is verbal or physical. Take steps to defend yourself emotionally:

- You may need to withdraw from fraught or harmful situations that you know will only get worse.
- Defuse your own anger by talking it out with your church leaders or friends you trust.
- Plan an evening off. Criticism can really get to you after a while. It won't destroy you but it will 'terrorise' you if you allow it to dominate your perception of yourself and others. You begin to think, 'Well, I can understand Mrs Bloggs feeling that way, but what if *everyone* is thinking like her?' Take evasive action. The more up-tight you feel because of someone's insensitivity or hurtfulness, the harder it is to relax – and the more important it is to do so!
- Listen to God's defence of you: 'You are precious and honoured in my sight, and . . . I love you' (Isaiah 43:4).

NO HIDDEN MOTIVES

A noted Christian doctor has listed several emotions which produce disease in human beings. Heading the list is fear, followed by frustration, rage, resentment, hatred, jealousy, envy, self-centredness, and ambition. The one and only antidote that can save people from these, he says, is love. He would have approved of this prescription that Jesus gave his disciples:

> 'You have heard that it was said, "Love your neighbour and hate your enemy." But I tell you,

> Love your enemies and pray for those who persecute you, that you may be sons of your Father in heaven. He causes his sun to rise on the evil and the good, and sends rain on the righteous and the unrighteous. If you love those who love you, what reward will you get? Are not even the tax collectors doing that? And if you greet only your brothers, what are you doing more than others? Do not even pagans do that? Be perfect, therefore, as your heavenly Father is perfect.' *Matthew 5:43–48*

Let me tell you about some of the things I love. I love my wife, I love my children, I love my parents, friends and cream cakes. I love those chocolate eggs with the gooey bits in the middle. I love wine gums, old films (some new ones too), and I love sport.

But I don't love all those things in the same way! I don't love my wife in the same way that I love gooey chocolate eggs. The word has different meanings in different contexts. Sometimes we mean 'like' when we say 'love'. When Jesus said, 'love your enemies', he didn't mean, 'like your enemies'. He wasn't saying, 'when you meet that person who's been really rotten to your child at school and is always insulting your wife, you are to like him.' That would be asking us to play emotional gymnastics in a way that would soon have the men in white coats coming for us. To try to twist our emotions and thoughts towards liking someone we honestly don't, would be harmful, false to the reality of the situation, and ultimately destructive.

Let's be honest: I can't stand my enemy. I hate his guts! The things he does are mean, cowardly and selfish, and I just don't want to know him. So how do I square that with what Jesus is saying in this passage?

Jesus says to us, 'I want you to come to me, recognising that on your own you cannot like or love this person. And I want to fill you with *my* love for him.' Anybody can love the people they like. Jesus' revolutionary principle is that we should love even the people we *don't* like – and who don't like us. If we want to become like Christ, 'perfect' children of our Father in heaven, this is the only option open to us.

To be perfect means to be completely fulfilled, doing the job we were meant to do. When we love our enemies we are being the sort of people God meant us to be. If I find that one of the shelves in our living room has a screw missing and is coming off the wall, I'll search around for the screwdriver. I've got to get the one with the head that's the right shape and precisely the right size. If it fits the screw just perfectly, and the screwdriver fits into my hand perfectly, if I can get it in under the shelf perfectly, and it screws in perfectly, then the Greek word *teleios* would be a perfect description of my screwdriver. *Teleios* means complete, or perfect. It's the word Jesus uses here: 'Be perfect as your heavenly Father is perfect.' The screwdriver is exactly right for the job, doing exactly what it is meant to do and in the way that it should. When we love our enemies we are doing precisely what God wants us to do in the way he wants us to do it. We are complete, perfect.

Jesus is again homing in on motives. 'There are no free lunches' is a fairly well established principle in the business world. So when we see the managing director taking his rival out for a meal, painfully keeping up polite conversation and an ingratiating smile, you know there's a deal in the offing. He has a particular motive for loving his enemy. Jesus turns the 'no free lunches' principle on its head. My motive for loving my enemy should never be a pretence, in order to get something from him, nor should it be a subtle form of revenge – a way of making him feel awful about the way he's treated me. My motive must be simply that of obeying Jesus – I will love my enemy because I love Jesus.

So how do we do that? Love is not primarily what we feel, but what we do. The way to start to love our enemies is not to try to work up a nice feeling towards them, but to start treating them the way God wants us to. It means behaving towards them in a way which honours God. If you are a boss, this might mean that you start praying for the trade union official who's such a pain in the neck. (And vice versa!) You'll stop to say hello to him when you pass him on the stairs or in the lift. You'll remember the names of his children and ask how they are. And gradually your perception of him will change. Feelings follow the facts. Act as if you care about him, and you soon will.

Someone has put it well; 'It is not love when one simply draws a beautiful picture in one's soul and endows it with every perfection; rather this is love: to love people as we find them, and if they have weaknesses, to accept them with a heart filled with love.' (Quoted by Lloyd Cory, *Quotable quotations*. Wheaton: Victor Books, 1985.)

INSIDES THAT MATCH THE OUTSIDES

There's a parody of Longfellow's poem, *Hiawatha*, that leaves you totally confused about this guy's mittens: are they inside-out or outside-in?

A Modern Hiawatha

When he killed the Mudjokivis,
Of the skin he made him mittens,
Made them with the fur side inside,
Made them with the skin side outside.
He, to get the warm side inside,
Put the inside skin side outside;
He, to get the cold side outside,
Put the outside warm side inside,
That's why he put the fur side inside,
Why he put the skin side outside,
Why he turned them inside outside.

(*George A Strong*)

Jesus was concerned that our lives should be so much of a piece that there is no difference between what we seem to be and what we really are. The image of ourselves that we project to others should genuinely reflect what we are like inside. Our constant prayer should be: 'Lord, let my inside match my outside!'

Jesus said:

> 'Be careful not to do your "acts of righteousness" before men, to be seen by them. If you do, you will have no reward from your Father in heaven.
>
> So when you give to the needy, do not announce it with trumpets, as the hypocrites do in the synagogues and on the streets, to be honoured by men. I tell you the truth, they have received their reward in full. But when you give to the needy do not let your left hand know what your right hand is doing, so that your giving may be in secret. Then your Father, who sees what is done in secret, will reward you.'

Matthew 6:1–4

Inside giving

There are two quite different aspects to the Christian life. One is the external, 'doing' or 'good works' aspect. The other is the inner relationship with God. In this bit of his sermon, Jesus shows how we can easily allow the two to drift apart, keeping up the show of a life lived in harmony with God and in obedience to him, yet in reality that being far from the truth.

It's clear from what Jesus says here that he expects his disciples to be giving to the needy, otherwise he'd have said, 'If you give . . .' not 'When you give . . .' People who live under the rule of God are going to be the sort of people who give to others, care about the oppressed and get bothered when they see people in need.

What does it mean to make our 'insides' match our 'outsides' in the area of giving?

- It means being reflective *and* active. Evangelical Christianity is known for its emphases on the need to be born again, to keep up a committed prayer life and to read the Bible daily. All those things are good, but there is a danger that we can be so absorbed in this 'reflective' side of Christianity that Jesus' commands to care for the hurting go unheard. We neglect the more active aspect of Christianity. I find it very easy to be so preoccupied in reading, prayer or preaching that I forget the needs of those outside the kingdom. We can simply fail to notice that someone needs the loving hand of a Christian individual reaching out to meet his needs in a practical way. Jesus reminds us of our responsibility, as his representatives, towards those in need in our communities.

- It means maintenance *and* mission. Tunnel vision can afflict whole churches as well as individual Christians. We can become inward-looking as churches. Sometimes we need to ask ourselves how many of our structures are designed with our own needs in mind and to make us feel good, and how much of our time, work, effort and vision we give as a church to those outside the kingdom. As we experience God, come to church regularly, continue in our faith year in year out, we can take for granted our relationship with Jesus Christ. We can become blasé and casual about all that the Lord has given us. Yet 'out there', not so far out there, either, are thousands in our community who are desperately searching for something that will give their lives meaning and purpose. They busy themselves with their families or bury themselves in work – or sometimes in drugs and alcohol – just to blot out the insistent questions that bother them in any moment of silence or aloneness: 'What's the purpose of all this? So you *are* earning more than last year, so your family *is* better off – but what's the point? Is it day after day of just the same all the way until the children leave home and it's just the two of us again, and then there are grandchildren and then we die? Is that all there is?'

It is this kind of need Jesus expects his followers to do something about too; not just the practical, physical needs for enough to eat, somewhere to live, and work to do.

- It means global *and* local. It's not too hard to be caught up in all the emotion of an international appeal for aid, and give generously to something like 'Live-Aid'. There are lots of big, national crises that cry out for our money and gifts of clothing and medicines. And it is right that we should give as generously as we can to these 'outside' concerns. But we should take care that we are not at the same time ignoring needs closer to home, the 'inside' ones in our own community. We can be very concerned about the needs of those in Sudan, Romania or Iraq but neglect the needs of our own elderly parents or handicapped next-door neighbour.

- It means meeting needs 'in secret'. If you went into the temple area at Jerusalem you would come into a courtyard. In the courtyard was a little room set aside, called the Chamber of the Silent. No noise or chatter was allowed there. When you had a gift to bring for the needy, you would bring it into this room and leave it there. After you had gone, the priest would come and take the money to distribute it to those who were most in need. It was a gift given and received in secret – no one knew how much you were giving, the priest didn't know who had put what there, the giver didn't know who would receive it and the recipient didn't know who had given.

The Chamber of the Silent is a picture of how we are to give: in secret, not looking for any praise or reward, not making people feel 'beholden' to us.

Sometimes we like to get full value for money out of our giving. A big company gives a lot of money to a charity and there will be a photo of the hand-over in the local paper, with someone from the company holding up a huge replica cheque with the sum of x-thousand pounds clearly written on it for all to see. That company is hoping for some sort of commercial spin-off as the local community becomes more favourably disposed towards it.

- It means giving for God's glory, not our own. There have been a number of times when I've given to someone, anonymously, because I felt that's where God wanted my money to go. And sometimes I hear second or third hand about how much that money was needed and that it had arrived just at the right time. These have been some of the most thrilling moments of my life! It's great to be able to provide the answer to someone's prayer, and so be the cause of their giving glory to God.

Inside praying

Our society values the public performance. Television, which absorbs so much of our time, is all about image. Politics is often about a public performance; preaching can also be no more than a public performance. But the image and the performance are not what really matters. What is crucial is what a man or woman is on the inside, on their knees before God:

> 'But when you pray, do not be like the hypocrites, for they love to pray standing in the synagogues and on the street corners to be seen by men. I tell you the truth, they have received their reward in full. When you pray, go into your room, close the door and pray to your Father, who is unseen. Then your Father, who sees what is done in secret, will reward you. And when you pray, do not keep on babbling like pagans, for they think they will be heard because of their many words. Do not be like them, for your Father knows what you need before you ask him.'
>
> *Matthew 6:5–8*

The reason why there is so much bankruptcy in the corporate prayer life of many churches, is that there is bankruptcy in our individual prayer lives. When we have the chance to pray together, whether in church meetings or in house groups, prayer is often very, very hard going! There is no power or authority in our prayers because the group is simply pooling its bankruptcy. We have nothing to bring. There is an emptiness inside because we have neglected the private place with God.

What factors have contributed to this, and how can we restore the heart of our Christian lives – our secret walk with God? We need to make choices each day on a number of issues:

To pray or just to think about it?

Prayer is something we continually have to decide to do. We cannot just decide one day to 'pray better' or 'every day for an hour' and then do it. We need to take that decision again each day. It is time for us to stir ourselves into serious praying, as individuals and as churches. God works in our lives, bringing us to maturity and carrying out his purposes in the world, only in response to our prayer and commitment.

Time for God or no time left?

We live in a world where the private, devotional life has never been harder, because the pace of our lives and world, particularly the western world, is so rapid. The place for prayer – private communion with God – is squeezed out.

At the end of the last century, a man called F W Norwood was living in London and went to see a huge mansion that he was thinking of buying. It was in the process of being renovated and redecorated by its current owner. The workmen were hard at it as he wandered through room after room – dining rooms, leisure rooms, bedrooms, and rooms for a whole range of other things. When he had worked his way to the centre of the house he found a very small room where the builders were at work. 'What's happened here?' he asked. 'Oh,' they replied, 'this used to be the chapel where the family met for prayers; the owners want it turned into a living room.'

Norwood couldn't help being struck, even all those years ago, that in an already massive house, with a room for every purpose, even the smallest room once set aside for prayer was being turned into a living room. In the heart of modern man and modern woman, the room for God is rapidly being squeezed out by the busyness of the process of living. In the centre of our lives, where God wants to be, there is nothing but a continual rush and bustle of activity. In the heart where there should be peace and a centring down on God, there is the same frantic activity that there is at the periphery of our lives.

In the words of C S Lewis, we are breeding men and women with no chests, no heart, no inner reality. (See C S Lewis, *The Abolition of Man*. London: Fount Publications, 1984.) We are all periphery, all edge, all activity. Sometimes we say that we can't get to the bottom of someone, we can't fathom them. But modern men and women are like onions: you peel them away one layer after another – and find you have peeled them away entirely! There is simply nothing of substance at their core.

Many Christians live at that level. They go to church, they pray, they worship, they may even attempt evangelism, but in their hearts there is no true heart. The hidden reality, the inner room with God, the moment by moment truth of the Christian faith, is tragically absent. The oyster remains but the pearl is gone.

What is at the core of your life? If everything were stripped away from you, your husband or wife, your family, wealth, job, would God still be there, at the very centre of your being? Make sure you have that quiet, inner place set apart for God.

And what about our church fellowships? If we stripped away the excitement of Sunday worship, the preaching, teaching, the activities of the various organisations, the structures that give it all shape, would we find a heart that pulsates with God? Would we find anything there at all?

Professional distance or personal commitment?

Helmut Thielicke, a German theologian who died a few years ago, warned that preachers were often the most guilty of inner emptiness. He described them as building houses for their congregations to live in: houses with foundations of biblical study, walls of prayer, a roof of church attendance and windows of evangelism. It's a good description of the shape our Christian living should take. Yet, Thielicke said, the preachers weren't living in those houses themselves. He didn't hesitate to call this hypocrisy. It's the trap of 'professionalism', the belief that it's my job to know all about a subject, but I don't need to be personally committed to it. I can stand outside it and advise people about it without having to get 'personally involved'.

Everyone who leads, speaks or teaches in the church is in danger of making their role a 'professional' one only. Each time we encourage others to do something that we are not doing ourselves, there is a conflict between our inner self and our outer self. The Baptist hymn book has a great hymn which says, 'Awake, O Lord, as in the time of old . . . Make us to be what we profess to be; from unreality set us free.' We need to pray that God will set us free from any trace of unreality, and that what we are in public and what we are in our private devotions are identical.

Trusting or bargaining?
Again and again in the Gospels, Jesus reveals that God is the loving Father of all who accept Jesus as Lord. That fact of God's fatherhood determines how we relate to him. Trust is in, bargaining is out. 'So don't get the idea,' says Jesus, 'that prayer is some sort of arm-twisting ritual: "Look, God, I really want this and that, and I'll say so three hundred times just to prove it!" Don't think of God like that,' Jesus says, 'he is your loving Father; he heard you the first time! And he wants to give you everything that is good.'

Campbell Morgan used to say, 'Prayer is laying hold of God's willingness, not overcoming his reluctance.' Prayer isn't about manipulating God into giving us the answer we want. It's about bringing to him, with the straightforward trust of a little child, all that is on our mind and laying it out before him. As we grow in prayer in the secret place of our hearts and understand more about what he wants, we will see more and more how willing God is to respond.

Inside fasting

> 'When you fast, do not look sombre as the hypocrites do, for they disfigure their faces to show men they

> are fasting. I tell you the truth, they have received their reward in full. But when you fast, put oil on your head and wash your face, so that it will not be obvious to men that you are fasting, but only to your Father, who is unseen; and your Father, who sees what is done in secret, will reward you.'
>
> *Matthew 6:16–18*

Here is another area where our insides should match our outsides – in more ways than one! The modern equivalent of 'disfiguring their faces to show men they are fasting' is to turn up to the mid-week prayer meeting after a day of fasting, not having shaved, looking pretty dishevelled, wearing a hang-dog sort of look – just to make sure everyone knows you've been very spiritual today!

For us to fast for a day is almost nothing in comparison with what was common practice for many people in the past. We do it so badly, and so rarely, that we make an enormous deal of it. Even though we might not let other people know – perhaps we dress smartly and don't tell anyone at all that we're fasting – inside we might be on a spiritual 'high', saying to ourselves, 'Lord, you must be delighted with me! I've fasted all day today! You just can't believe your luck with a Christian like me, can you?'

Well, it's better not to fast at all than to have that attitude! We're not meant to fast for our own benefit, nor for a reward, but because our whole life is given over to God and committed to him. Fasting is symbolic of that and is a natural consequence of it.

Fasting has been part of committed Christian witness down through the ages. Generally speaking, this century has seen less of it than perhaps any other –

certainly in western Europe – and only in the last twenty years or so has much been written and said about it in Protestant circles. Fasting should accompany our prayers, not to show how spiritual we are nor to get a warm spiritual glow, but as a way of saying that we are really serious about a particular issue. Just as we lose our appetite naturally when we are churned up inside about something, so the decision to fast should reflect a genuine 'churning up' inside about something in particular. It might be that you are desperately concerned to see the forces of evil bound, and their power over our social structures evaporate. Perhaps you really want to see your church move on in its praise and worship.

There are frequent occasions in the Old Testament when a fast was called. It was usually in response to a crisis – perhaps an army was invading (2 Chronicles 20:3–4), or because a daunting and difficult task was about to be undertaken and the people wanted to commit it to God (Ezra 8:21), or because the people had become aware of a particular sin in their lives and wanted to show their repentance from it (Jeremiah 36:1–10). Today, perhaps we do not fast more as churches, small groups and individuals, because we do not feel so strongly about the forces that threaten to disrupt God's church and ruin his world. On the outside we claim to be concerned, but is that claim matched by real concern on the inside?

Let us ask God to give us a glimpse of the world from his perspective, and to feel about it as he does. Then our prayers will take on a new life and integrity, and will be marked with a new urgency and effectiveness.

7

HANDLING THE PRESSURE

Some days are better than others. Take the first day of your summer holiday for example: the day you've been looking forward to for the last three months. You wake up and what do you hear? Rain pattering on the windows. And perhaps a rumble of thunder. You discover that the kids have already been fighting for hours. When the sun eventually comes out and the car is packed up for the two weeks' holiday, can you get it started? Of course not. The hamster dies of fright as soon as you arrive with it at Mrs Jones', and you have to spend two hours explaining everything about heaven to a little cluster of tearful children. You vow you will never again try to spend a holiday anywhere other than at home!

There must have been a few days when the disciples wondered just what they were doing. 'Who is this Jesus? Have we really done the right thing, selling up and leaving home for the sake of this man?'

Jesus knew what they were thinking. He knew they were under a lot of pressure because of their decision to be with him. And he knew that this pressure would only increase for them after his death, resurrection and ascension. So he gave them a prayer that drew together all their main sources of worry and tension, allowing them to acknowledge the reality of their fears and then to lay them all at the feet of their Father in heaven:

> 'This is how you should pray:
>
> "Our Father in heaven,
> hallowed be your name,
> your kingdom come,
> your will be done
>   on earth as it is in heaven.
> Give us today our daily bread.
> Forgive us our debts,
>   as we also have forgiven our debtors.
> And lead us not into temptation,
>   but deliver us from the evil one." '
>
> *Matthew 6:9–13*

MY FATHER, IN CONTROL

There is a story about a Roman emperor, returning to Rome in victory after a long war. His wife and children were watching the triumphal procession from a raised dias. Suddenly one of his little boys rushed down through the crowd, pushing through people's legs, and ran out into the main parade. He was grabbed by a Roman soldier and yanked back. 'Where do you think you're going?' he demanded of the boy. 'That's the Emperor you were heading for!' The little boy replied, 'He may be your emperor, but he's my father!'

That's the picture the Lord's Prayer gives us: it has all the weight and solemnity of addressing an emperor, but all the trust and intimacy of running up to a loving father. To those who belong to Christ, God is not a distant despot, the Dictator of the universe; he is a gentle, loving, approachable Father.

It's difficult for us to realise what a revelation this would have been to the disciples. They had been brought up, as all Jews would have, to believe that God's name was so holy you mustn't even say it. After all, God had not even told Moses his name. When Moses had asked what it was, God had simply replied, 'I am who I am' (Exodus 3:14).

Jesus puts things on a different footing. He doesn't focus on the distance between God and people, but on a relationship. God is our Father because we have been born into his family. The Lord's prayer becomes ours when we become Christians. Nowhere does the Bible say that God is the Father of every person in the world. He is the Father of those who have come to him in faith through Jesus.

What a lovely image! Those who have been badly treated by their human fathers have in God a Father who is totally good, kind and perfect. A young mum might be bringing up children on her own without the influence and support of their earthly father, perhaps because of divorce or bereavement. In God they have the perfect Father-figure. He can come into that painful situation and be the father those children never had and the supporting husband that the wife has lost.

Approachable, caring, loving – yet also fatherly in his discipline of his children. I wouldn't be much of a father if I didn't discipline my three children. One thing parents seem to disagree over more than almost anything else, is about how much discipline is necessary. In our house the arguments go something like this:

'Don't shout at them – they couldn't help it!'
'Yes they could!'
'No they couldn't; you've got to make allowances for the fact that they're tired.'
'Why should I? That was still naughty . . .'

As parents we worry about the discipline of our children. As our Father, God worries about our discipline, in the sense of being concerned, bothered. He's not a doddery old fool whom we can con; he's a Father with enormous discernment who knows us through and through, and who has absolute authority over us. His discipline of us is always right on target, exactly what we need; neither too little nor too much, and always at just the right time.

And this Father is also King. He is 'in heaven', on the throne of the whole world. What a relief that is! So often we can feel real anger and despair when we read the papers and see the TV news. The world is such a desperately evil place, there are times when we wish we were out of it. International terrorism, petty squabbles between super-powers that suddenly assume an awful importance, more hostages taken, aeroplanes hijacked, another tornado and an earthquake, thousands more deaths in Africa from famine and AIDS. Tensions mount and the whole world looks terminally sick. Jesus himself warned his disciples that things would stay looking pretty bad: 'There will be wars and rumours of wars . . . Nation will rise against nation, and kingdom against kingdom. There will be earthquakes in various places, and famines . . . those days will be days of distress unequalled from the beginning . . .' (Mark 13:7–8, 19). Yet in the light of all that, he could still teach his disciples to say, 'Our Father, in heaven – in control.'

There is a limit to which Satan will be allowed to operate. There is a limit to the level to which God will allow the world to descend. Ultimately the destiny of our planet does not depend on its political leaders. Ultimate power lies in the hands of the living, loving God. That is a fact which we grasp by faith as we come to know God as our Father, and gradually begin to perceive how he is at work in the world.

HONOUR WHERE HONOUR'S DUE

'Hallowed' is not a word we use very often! 'Honour' is the idea behind it. God is to be honoured, taken seriously, respected. There were many idols and images of gods around in the first century, all of which were honoured to a greater or lesser degree. But they were simply lumps of wood, stone or metal; they weren't remotely worthy of being honoured.

But God is real, and his greatness should challenge our tendency to be flippant about him. Much of today's popular humour is flippant and destructive. It's hard to know where to draw the line. I find much 'alternative humour' really funny, but it sometimes pushes the boundaries back too far. Humour can push back boundaries of acceptability that nothing else can budge. When the satirists started poking fun at politics, none of us minded too much. On the whole, we probably felt that the politicians got what they deserved. Then they began poking fun at religion, but it was usually stuffy old services and weird vicars who came in for it, so again we didn't mind that either. Then they began to poke fun at God. And even that wasn't too bad because it was people's caricatures of God that were being demolished. We felt quite safe with that because we didn't actually believe those things about God. But when Jesus, his life, death and resurrection become the source of amusement and entertainment, and the very heart of all that we stand for is ridiculed and pooh-poohed, we suddenly find ourselves exposed, caught out.

Humour can be far more dangerous than antagonism or persecution. Those things produce martyrs; humour and ridicule simply make us look idiots. Yet we often take ourselves too seriously. It is our own reputations that we're usually concerned for, not God's.

And that spills over into our church life. The insidious influence of public satire, and our own pompous concern for our 'image', lead us almost to 'downgrade' God. Our attitude to corporate worship can become casual, even irreverent. When we gather together, we come to honour our special guest, the king of the universe, who has promised to be with us. Yet we find it hard not to be distracted. We have irrelevant chats with people about nothing at all, and can slide into thinking of Sunday worship as 'just another service' rather than an incredible opportunity to meet with our great king, the living God.

A LITTLE BIT OF HEAVEN NOW

Life is a bit like a story in which the characters inside it are always trying to guess how it will end. But no-one stuck inside a story that is happening can possibly say what the outcome will be. Neither can they tell what the point of it all is. We can only know that, if someone from outside the story lets us in on the secret. The Bible tells us that this is precisely what has happened in our world. We have been 'let in on the secret' of what it's all about and how it will end. It's what we call 'revelation'. What we're shown is that, at the end of the story, God's kingdom will be firmly established on this earth. Everything else in life may be uncertain, but this fact is absolutely beyond doubt.

Jesus told his disciples to pray that it would happen sooner rather than later: 'Your kingdom come, your will be done on earth as it is in heaven.' In other words, 'pray that the reign and rule of God in heaven, a reign which is perfect and total, will begin to manifest itself on earth now, so that heaven will happen here more and more.' That's the whole point of the story: that Jesus Christ, the king of heaven in human form, will be given the kingship and bring all people under his rule.

Praying for God's kingdom to come is what we do every time we intercede with God on behalf of others. We're inviting the Jesus who rules in heaven to bring about here on earth the same situation that already exists in heaven. When we ask for the forgiveness of sin, we're asking that it will be taken away as it's already been taken away in heaven. When we pray for healing we're asking that there will be wholeness of body, mind and spirit, as there is in heaven. We pray that heaven may touch earth and spread its power and influence throughout it.

The ministry of intercession is an exciting one! It's praying God's power out of heaven into earth, asking for the joy, peace, healing, forgiveness and wholeness of heaven to become more and more apparent here, both in our church family and in the whole world. What a great thing to pray for!

DAILY RENEWAL

The next bit of the Lord's prayer seems totally out of place. After that magnificent glimpse at the great sweep of world history, Jesus seems to be saying, 'And, God, if we could have lunch every day, that would be nice. Give us today our daily bread.'

The Greek word used for 'daily' only appears in the New Testament in the context of the Lord's prayer. It doesn't come anywhere else. It's an unusual word and, for years, scholars didn't know what to make of it. Then some archaeologists found an ancient shopping list, dating from the first century, written in Greek. This word, 'daily' appeared beside a number of items on the shopping list. It could, perhaps, have meant 'large size' or 'on special offer', but the archaeologists decided it was more likely to mean, 'you've got to get this stuff each day.' Some of the items on the list could be bought and stored for a month or so, but other things, with this special word written alongside them, would go off quickly. They had to be bought fresh each day.

To the Jews, then, the request, 'Give us today our daily bread' was a very simple, practical prayer. But it packs a big punch! Behind its simplicity is a tremendous truth that many of us fail to grasp. People in the 1990s, and many Christians among them, are either living in the past or in the future! We thank God for what he gave us yesterday, for his blessing and for filling us with his Spirit, and we live our Christian lives in the strength of those past blessings. Or we live in hope for tomorrow. 'Maybe tomorrow will be better. Maybe I'll get those things done then. As soon as I've got into that new job I'll be able to spend time properly with my family.' We need instead to live in 'today', the place of daily blessing that God longs for us to know.

We might have had all sorts of great experiences of God in the past, but they were for then, not now. We might have been filled with God at one time, our lives radiating his love. When we went to church God's presence was real, we could almost feel him! Witnessing was no problem and life seemed to be one long, intimate conversation with the king. But, somehow, that has gone flat and stale on us, like a bottle of fizzy lemonade that has lost its fizz and taste. If we live on yesterday's spiritual bread our spiritual lives will go flat and not be very tasty.

We need God's blessing and provision each day. God longs to give us this daily renewal in his service; let's come to him each day to receive it.

CLEARING OUT THE CELLARS

God is in heaven. He is all-powerful and worthy of being worshipped. His kingdom will most certainly come. But if we want his will to be done on earth as it's being done in heaven, and if we want our daily bread, God's blessing for today, there is a big problem. Something stands in the way of that happening. That is why Jesus tells us to come to God and say:

> ' "Forgive us our debts, as we also have forgiven our debtors . . ." For if you forgive men when they sin against you, your heavenly Father will also forgive you. But if you do not forgive men their sins, your Father will not forgive your sins.'
>
> *Matthew 6:12, 14–15*

There is a stark principle here. If we don't grasp it and put it into practice, we'll be unable to receive the daily, fresh anointing that God wants to give us. The principle is simply that God calls on us to forgive those who have hurt, wronged or abused us, in whatever way.

Over the years an amazing quantity of hurts, fears and damage can accumulate in our lives. It builds up like toxic waste, but because it is usually too painful to live with we stuff it all down below in the cellars of our minds and hearts. And there it festers away, poisoning the way we respond to other people, damaging the way we view ourselves and crippling our spiritual development. But there is also some particularly poisonous stuff that we put there too, stacking it in neat, careful rows: unforgiveness and bitterness. Jesus is adamant that we need to clear out this bitterness; it's a spiritual and emotional health hazard. If we don't, we'll be the losers, for two reasons.

Firstly, bitterness eats away at our spirits like a cancer. When I was a student pastor I was placed in a church just outside Bedford. One of the church leaders there said something to me that I felt was quite unjustified. I was very hurt by it and angry with him. I didn't say anything at the time, but I brooded on it. Over a matter of months I found myself getting angrier and angrier about this person's attitude to me. And then I began to catch myself wishing bad things on him. If he wasn't at church on a Sunday I'd hope it wasn't just for some trivial reason but that he'd got his 'just desserts'.

That's a dreadful condition to be in. Unforgiveness destroys ourselves and our relationships with others in the family of God. God calls us to a revolution in our ideas and practice of forgiveness.

Secondly, while we continue to be unforgiving, we allow the person who hurt us, and his or her action, to carry on having a hold over us. It's like being trapped emotionally while the resentment, grief and bitterness work away inside. In a book that looks at the stories of people who have been abused, the author describes one young woman who hated her father because of the way he had damaged her. The author comments:

> 'The strange paradox of the whole matter is that until she forgives her father, he (though now in prison) has the power to go on ruining her life. When she makes the choice to forgive him, his power over her life is destroyed.'

And she adds, 'The key of forgiveness is a heavy one, and it is a painful struggle to turn it in rusty locks.' (Maxine Hancock and Karen Burton Mains, *Child Sexual Abuse: A hope for healing*. Crowborough: Highland Books, 1990.)

It is a hard principle. Gandhi recognised this when he said, 'The weak can never forgive. Forgiveness is an attribute of the strong.' This strength can come only from a deep sense of security in God. When we know he is our Father, that we are infinitely precious to him and that nothing will shake his love for us, we can reach out to others with forgiveness, without fear of being diminished.

I wonder who it is in your life that you most need to forgive. Perhaps your wife who criticises and nags you? Perhaps your husband whose attitude towards you is demeaning and humiliating? If you are in this situation, seek counsel and help from your church leaders to enable your relationship to get back on an even keel.

As parents we need sometimes to ask the forgiveness of our children. As children we may need to ask the forgiveness of our parents. There are colleagues who need to ask forgiveness of one another; church leaders and church members who need to say sorry to God and one another. Forgiveness is the key to spiritual release and blessing.

SAVE ME FROM THE MONSTERS

Satan can be a real pain, constantly looking for ways of tripping us up, appearing as an angel of light – and we can be so gullible! Even if he worked only part time he'd probably still trip most of us up. We have to be so alert to the work of the evil one. His job is to bring division, gossip and condemnation into God's family; God's job is to bring brothers and sisters together again. Satan's job is to make us feel disgusted and depressed with our spiritual lives. God's job is to point out the sin and then to forgive and restore us. It's Satan's job to sow doubt, fear and tension; it's God's role to bring certainty, wholeness and a relaxation in his presence.

Satan is at work in our lives, our churches and our land. Before we know it, we've been caught in his trap and suddenly find ourselves dangling helplessly and miserably from the monster's jaws. We need to pray to be delivered from temptation and protected from evil.

Such prayers are prayed by realists, people who know themselves and have no illusions about their own strength. God does sometimes allow us to go through difficult times to test and strengthen our faith. But that doesn't mean we should *ask* for such testing. Peter Kreeft, an American theologian and philosopher, explains it like this:

> 'Compare the following two prayers . . . (1) "Lord, I thank thee that I am not like other men. I can and will endure heroic sufferings for you. Please send them my way"; and (2) "God be merciful to me, a sinner. I am weak. I can hardly endure even a little pain for you. Therefore, please do not send me great pain."
>
> Self-delusion prays, "I am strong." Self-knowledge says, "I am weak." Self-knowledge says, "I am riddled with evils – physical, psychological, and spiritual, as with bullets or cancer. Therefore, I need deliverance. Deliver me from evil." ' (Peter Kreeft, 'Tribulation within limits', *Christianity Today*, 16 May 1986. Carol Stream: Christianity Today Inc.)

The IRA has a motto: 'England's difficulty is our opportunity.' In February 1991 during the Gulf War, the IRA exploited the fact that the cabinet was totally preoccupied with the Gulf War, and launched a mortar bomb at Number 10, Downing Street. In the same way, Satan is an opportunist who exploits our weaknesses. We are either fools or fatally proud if we do not realise this and ask for God's protection.

INTO NEW DIMENSIONS

What is your prayer life like? If your parents were Christians you were probably taught to pray as you grew up. My mother used to come into my bedroom at bed time, kneel down by my bedside holding my hand, and say, 'Now, let's pray.' And we'd say, 'Jesus, tender shepherd, hear me, bless thy little lambs tonight.' For a while that was fine, but eventually I got bothered by these lambs; I couldn't work out where they were. Then our prayer would go on: 'God bless Grandma and Grandad, and the other Grandad and Grandma . . .' (I never knew which was which, but it didn't seem to matter) '. . . and Mummy and Daddy and Sue.' And then we'd say a prayer at the end about something different each day.

Now that was right and good – I'm not knocking it at all. But I suspect that, years later, many of us simply put adult phrases on that same model and are carrying on praying in exactly the same way. We're still saying nothing much more than, 'God bless Grandma and Grandad; God look after this and God do that; God help me at work tomorrow and please give me a better day. And if you could arrange a rise in salary . . .'

I believe God is calling us out of that immaturity into new levels and dimensions of prayer. The devil is more concerned about our praying than about any other aspect of our living. That's why the church prayer meeting is often the last thing to be revitalised. If we really want to see God's kingdom come and his will done on earth, as it is in heaven, we must understand that this will not happen simply through the vehicles of worship or evangelism. It is only the serious praying of the people of God that will bring it about.

8

ULTIMATE COMMITMENT

Throughout the centuries, people have worried about what might happen should they suddenly fall on hard times. In the twentieth-century western world we expect life to give us more than ever before, and our concern for the future has a new complication: we believe that the ultimate aim in life is to be happy. So we take every step we can to make sure of our present and future happiness. We scrutinise the adverts of the banks and building societies to see which one will be able to give us the biggest nest egg on our retirement. We don't want to get caught out by sudden redundancy or illness, so we save up for that 'rainy day'.

As Jesus' disciples and all the hangers-on sat or stood nearby to listen to him, he gave them some advice on sound investments against the ultimate 'rainy day':

> 'Do not store up for yourselves treasures on earth, where moth and rust destroy, and where thieves break in and steal. But store up for yourselves treasures in heaven, where moth and rust do not destroy, and where thieves do not break in and steal. For where your treasure is, there your heart will be also.' *Matthew 6:19–21*

As Jesus looked around at the crowd he would have seen fishermen, farmers, lawyers, probably Roman soldiers too. To each one he directed the same question: 'Where is your treasure?' He was talking about far more than money. 'What is it that really matters to you?' was his meaning. 'What are you living for? What's your aim, your goal in life? Where are you heading? What is it that you're prepared to sacrifice for? Because in that place where you've committed everything – time, money, effort, imagination, will – that's where your heart's going to be. What you devote your life to will ultimately define who you are as a person. So it's important to know what your goals and desires are. Fishermen, is your goal to catch more and bigger fish? Farmers, is it to have more crops and own more land? Religious lawyers, is it to know more of the Law by heart and stun people with your wisdom? Soldiers, is your aim to get promoted from the ranks to be centurions?'

This is a bit of Jesus' questioning we feel we can skip as Christians. After all, the answer is obvious, isn't it? 'My treasure is in heaven, of course! Why don't you ask non-Christians that question? They're the ones with their lives all wrapped up in these earthly things!'

Well, that may be true. But as Christians who have made a commitment to Jesus and known the touch of his hand on our lives, we are equally prone to keeping God on the edges of our lives. There are Christians who are so absorbed in the process of 'getting on' in their careers that they have failed to get on in the kingdom. Ambition is not wrong. It is good to want to be the best teacher, accountant or worker on the shop floor. But the reason for our ambition needs to be looked at carefully. Ambition is bad when our aim is to be seen, praised and admired for being such a wonderful person. Our aim then is not really to be 'the best teacher', or whatever, but 'to be well-known and admired'.

Many of us claim the Lordship of Christ over our lives, but in practical terms we are more committed to our careers, homes, or some other physical thing. How can we tell, honestly, what our aim is in life? Try the burglary test: what would you miss most if it were taken away from you? The TV or video? For many of us our leisure time is more dominated by these things than we would like to admit. What about our career? If that was taken from us would life still have meaning for us? What about our family? It could happen. What about our reputation in the local community? Are we prepared for that to suffer for the sake of Christ?

WORLD AT WAR

Perhaps we would see our daily life in clearer perspective if we reminded ourselves that we are in the middle of a war. Many Christians live a leisurely life in the kingdom as though it were peace time. The recruits turn up occasionally for combat exercises with the commander in chief, and they go through various drill routines Sunday by Sunday. But basically, they do much as they like during the rest of the week.

The kingdom of God is a battleground, not a playground. That is why God's first concern is not for our happiness but for our wisdom and maturity. The call to Christian conversion is a call to engage in spiritual warfare with the kingdom of darkness. The fact that there is a 'kingdom of God' implies that there is an area outside it, opposed to it.

We are caught up in a war whether we like it or not. The only choice we have is which side we're going to be on! As members of God's kingdom we're involved in a fight against evil social structures, against Satan's activity in the world, against our own sinfulness, and against any number of problems in society that arise from people's sinfulness. What are we investing in this battle? Are we spending so much time and effort investing in things of this world that will soon be as insignificant as dust, that we leave no time to invest in things of eternal and lasting significance?

The *Queen Mary* is a large ship that has been used in peace time and in times of war. It is now docked just off the Californian coast and is a major tourist attraction. When you board it to see round, you come across its huge dining room, divided down the middle by a massive partition. On one side of the partition the tables are laid out as they were in peace time. The place settings are set a comfortable distance apart from each other, each with seven or eight plates and a myriad of cutlery. I wouldn't know where to begin with it! It's a bewildering display of opulence. One corner of that room has been made up as a bedroom suite, just to show what it would have been like. There's a four-poster bed, and an amazingly luxurious range of other furnishings.

Then there's the partition. On its other side the tables are set out as for war time. One metal tray marks each place. There's a hole in each tray for a cup, a little dent marking the place for the dessert, and a slightly bigger dent marking the place for the main course. Some of the places had a knife and a fork. The really lucky ones had a spoon, too! In the corner of this room, there is no four-poster bed but a five-tier bunk.

In war time the *Queen Mary* upped its complement from 3000 passengers to 15,000. Five times as many people, living in a completely different environment. One set of circumstances was appropriate for peace time, a completely different set for war time. As Christians, I believe we are often living on the wrong side of the partition. We need to bring all our efforts to bear on things that matter and will last.

POCKETS OF RESISTANCE

It's a well-known fact that the last part of a man to be converted is his pocket. We resist yielding totally to the call of God to be committed to him. We are complicated people who can easily deceive ourselves about our motives and goals, and we can unearth pockets of resistance in the most surprising places.

As a preacher, I can kid myself that I don't have a problem with false goals; of course my treasure's in godly things. I'm constantly about the king's business! But am I? Aren't I in great danger of being so much in love with the work of the Lord that I forget the Lord of the work? Some of us so enjoy worship that we forget the God we're worshipping. We can so much enjoy the fellowship and friendship of one another that the God who binds us together is somehow distanced. These are subtle temptations, but we are more prone to fall for them than we care to admit. 'My treasure in worldly things? Goodness, no! I've moved on from that;

my treasure is now in *religious* things!'

Jesus says both of these are wrong. He wants our treasure to be *him*, because when he has pride of place in our lives as our most precious possession, all other things in life will fall into their rightful places. It's not that these other things are bad; they're mostly good and necessary, but if we seek the King and his kingdom first, 'all these things will be given to you as well.'

Jesus went on to warn his listeners about the dangers of thinking, 'I'm OK; I don't need to bother about all this treasure stuff just now. I'll sort it out some other time.' Don't be fobbed off by this sort of thinking!

> 'The eye is the lamp of the body. If your eyes are good, your whole body will be full of light. But if your eyes are bad, your whole body will be full of darkness. If then the light within you is darkness, how great is that darkness!' *Matthew 6:22–23*

We need to see the real situation clearly. If we don't, how utterly blind we will be! If we can't see what the most important thing in life is, how on earth will we be able to see anything else clearly? We'll be condemned to wander around in this life like blind people, not sure what we are doing, where we are going or why we are going there.

A divided heart

> 'No one can serve two masters. Either he will hate the one and love the other, or he will be devoted to the one and despise the other. You cannot serve both God and Money.' *Matthew 6:24*

If you've ever been in the situation of working for two

bosses, you'll know how difficult life can be! One comes along and asks you to do something and says it's very urgent; then the other rushes up and says, 'Please could you do this, *now*! It's really important!' Or they both give you horrible jobs and you don't want to do either of them. Or their conflicting demands mean that you don't get either job done properly so they both shout at you! Working for two masters is a real problem.

Even when we have committed ourselves wholeheartedly just to one master, Jesus Christ, we go on discovering pockets of resistance throughout our lives. It's as though we have to be converted bit by bit. When Richard the Lionheart came back from the Crusades, he found that Prince John had set up a series of rival kingdoms within the kingdom. Some people were loyal to him. He'd been telling them that Richard would certainly be killed in the Crusades, or at least be there for years – being such a religious fanatic. 'So follow me', he said, 'and I'll give you a nice little kingdom to rule over. How would Durham suit you?' So when Richard returned he found the kingdom divided into a number of different mini-kingdoms. With the assistance of his army he mopped up most of the south coast resistance fairly quickly, but areas of rebellion remained, staunchly fortified with castles. The only way to defeat them was for Richard to lay siege to each one in turn, defeat the defenders and take it over.

There are many areas of our lives which we have not yet handed over to the King. We are perhaps not so up-front about it with God as Prince John was with Richard, but we have little private domains in our lives, little castles where we put our money or possessions, sexuality, time, job or something else, and try to keep them for ourselves. We don't want God to take control of that area of our lives. And because we're not fully God's, we aren't free to worship him in the way he deserves to be worshipped. We can't be free to share our faith as we ought to. We're not free to read the Bible, pray and grow as Christians. The internal struggle caused by those castles of rebellion brings tension, pain, emotional imbalance, stress and spiritual agony.

Taking back the areas of resistance

Set aside a chunk of time, perhaps an hour, and sit down with God to think over these questions:

- What do I really want out of life?
- What do I want to have achieved in ten years' time?
- How do I want to be different in ten years' time from the person I am now?
- What do I use these things for most:
  - my money?
  - my time?
  - my energy?
  - my imagination?

As you answer these questions honestly, ask God to show you how you could invest more in his kingdom. Ask for a new awareness of the king, Jesus, calling you to be with him and to share in all that he does, as he goes out to battle.

It would be helpful to talk this over with a friend in your house group or church, or with your church leaders. We need the encouragement of one another, and it helps us keep our commitment to Jesus fresh if we know someone else knows that we've made it!

GOD'S COMMITMENT TO US

We're in a battle, sure enough. But, says Jesus, 'don't worry!' I've always thought that's a great deal easier to say than it is to do. But just as we have committed ourselves to God, so he has committed himself to us.

> 'Therefore I tell you, do not worry about your life, what you will eat or drink; or about your body, what you will wear. Is not life more important than food, and the body more important than clothes? Look at the birds of the air; they do not sow or reap or store away in barns, and yet your heavenly Father feeds them. Are you not much more valuable than they? Who of you by worrying can add a single hour to his life?
>
> And why do you worry about clothes? See how the lilies of the field grow. They do not labour or spin. Yet I tell you that not even Solomon in all his splendour was dressed like one of these. If that is how God clothes the grass of the field, which is here today and tomorrow is thrown into the fire, will he not much more clothe you, O you of little faith?'
>
> *Matthew 6:25–30*

Worry can't change anything. How many of the things you've worried about have actually happened? Probably about one per cent. How many circumstances have you managed to change by worrying about them? None. We'd all have to admit that Jesus' logic is impeccable – but still we keep on worrying! Jesus reaches out to you today and says, 'You worry so much! Don't you know that you've got a heavenly Father who knows your needs and who loves you?'

Jesus has good reason to tell us to stop worrying. He's not saying it just to gloss over our discomfort and fear, but because it's illogical, not sensible and won't achieve anything. And there's another good reason not to worry: of all people, we are most blessed. We have a Father who knows our needs and who cares for us. In a world where worry is endemic, we've got somewhere to run and hide, somewhere to go and to be secure.

One afternoon we took Bethany to a little farm on the outskirts of Preston. She was about two at the time. The farmer's daughter took us to see a litter of week-old piglets. There were about twenty of them, and as we walked up to them they suddenly began to screech! Bethany had run on ahead but leapt back in fear, flung herself into my arms and almost throttled me. She wouldn't so much as look at them! So I said, 'Darling, the pigs can't get out, you're perfectly safe.' But by this time Bethany was making almost as much noise as the pigs! She was terrified.

You and I hear all the screeching and squealing of tomorrow, and we're terrified of what might happen – at work, with our health, in our job, with our family. And the devil turns up the volume so that we're even more afraid! But God is holding us securely in his arms, saying, 'Look, they can't get out, they can't get to you except through me. They can't hurt you; I'm your Father.'

Of course, bad things do happen to God's people. Tensions, problems and difficulties do come our way. But we're given the gift of a Father who says, 'I care for the sparrows – and you can pick those up for 10p down the market! And I love them. I make the grass grow (and don't we know it!); I clothe it with its colours and its seeds, and yet I love you countless millions times more than the grass! Don't worry. I even hear it when a sparrow falls from the sky. So don't be anxious; you're surrounded with my love and compassion.'

> 'So do not worry saying, "What shall we eat?" Or "What shall we drink?" Or "What shall we wear?" For the pagans run after all these things, and your heavenly Father knows that you need them. But seek first his kingdom and his righteousness, and all these things will be given to you as well. Therefore do not worry about tomorrow, for tomorrow will worry about itself. Each day has trouble enough of its own.'
>
> *Matthew 6:31–34*

Have you ever met a great man or woman of faith, the sort who seem so sold out to God that their lives are totally absorbed in him and his kingdom? Yet somehow all the practical details of their lives seem to get sorted out, too. Their problems have a way of working themselves out, while you and I get four or five ulcers a week worrying about whether that is going to fall into place, or whether this is going to happen, and whether I remembered to do that. It's a struggle! But for those folk who seem to be committed to God's kingdom almost to the point of recklessness, the practicalities of their lives often seem incredibly well ordered. I believe this is a promise which God honours literally, that when we put the kingdom first, other things will fall into place.

For some of us the answer to our worry and need is to change our focus. We should no longer look on the problems that cause us to worry, but look on Jesus and ask him to fill us with a vision of himself.

I vividly remember a time when I was a young

child of about eight. I was out with my family late one evening walking through the countryside, and I had run on ahead of the others. Suddenly a huge dog came racing out of the darkness towards me and stopped abruptly in the middle of the path, barking and baring its teeth. I stood there paralysed with fear, not knowing whether to run, or if that would make it chase me, or whether to pray that I would die or that it would die! I didn't know what to do. And then my father, walking up behind and past me, stood by the dog. I have a mental picture of the dog suddenly shrinking in size, my father seemed so big in comparison. He went up to it and told it to clear off – or words to that effect! And the dog just ran away. My father seemed eighteen feet tall and the dog seemed like a midget! Some years later I told my father about that, and he confessed to having been terrified too! But the dog went.

As I focused on my father the dog seemed to grow smaller, because my dad was in control. Today, you and I are surrounded by the wolves and vicious dogs of problems that snarl and snap at us, making us fearful and preventing us from going any further. Jesus calls us to turn our focus away from those dogs on to the Father standing next to them, who is big enough and powerful enough to make all those things look insignificant. The God who closed the lions' mouths for Daniel is big enough to close the mouth of the yapping dog.

Where is your treasure? Let us put it in the hands of our loving, powerful Father who can silence all the yapping dogs of the world with his presence.

9

SOUND JUDGMENT

One of the criticisms commonly aimed at Christians – particularly evangelical ones – is that they are all unthinking simpletons who have thrown out their brains in favour of a 'happy clappy' emotionalism. While this may be true of some people, the Bible emphasises that the chief characteristics of a godly life include wisdom, discernment, integrity and sound judgment.

In today's secular world, these words carry a whole range of different meanings. We can damn people with faint praise, smudge someone's character or initiate a less than honest deal, all in the interests of 'sound judgment' and 'discernment'. It is hard to separate truth from falsehood, even when trying to be clear about our own motives! So is it better to throw out our brains after all and just rely on a sort of 'holy instinct' to judge what is right and what is wrong?

Jesus' sermon gives some clear guidelines on how to judge and discern properly. He starts by drawing a clear distinction between right and wrong types of judgment:

> 'Do not judge, or you too will be judged. For in the same way you judge others, you will be judged, and with the measure you use, it will be measured to you.'
>
> *Matthew 7:1–2*

DESTRUCTIVE CRITICISM

We need to be clear first of all about what this passage is *not* saying. 'Judge' is used in two main ways in the New Testament. There are a number of Greek words for the idea of judging, but there are just two main groups of words. One of the groups uses it as in 'to condemn or criticise', and the other uses judge in the sense of, 'to make a decision'.

At Wimbledon they have installed electronic judges, so that when the ball is going at 100 miles per hour and the umpire can't see exactly what it's doing, a little bleep will tell him whether it was on the line, just outside the line, or just inside – so that he can make an informed decision. That judgment is a decision on how to act, based on a variety of facts. This is *not* how Jesus uses the word here. He's not saying, 'don't be discerning', but 'don't be condemning and critical', the kind of person who, when she sees someone doing something she can't understand, appoints herself judge, council for the prosecution, and jury too! The force of his statement is, 'Don't *go on habitually* judging and criticising. That kind of lifestyle is wrong. From time to time we need to take stock of ourselves and ask, 'Am I a judgmental sort of person? Am I a critical person? Is my first statement in any situation negative?'

An American psychiatrist has made a study of the case-histories of 10,000 people who were mentally or emotionally ill, or in some other kind of mental pain. As they asked for his help, he divided them into two categories. The first was made up of those suffering from mental and emotional disturbances; the second contained those who were largely free from such tensions. Gradually, one fact began to stand out. Those who were in the 'nervous and neurotic' group were habitual fault-finders, constantly critical of the people and things around them. Whereas those who were free from these tensions were the least fault-finding. His conclusion was that the habit of criticising others is related to mental imbalance.

Perhaps his conclusion is right, perhaps not. But if the art of continually criticising others does not indicate a state of mental imbalance, it would be fair to say it marks a state of spiritual imbalance.

When you think about it, the people you know who are good to be around are not those who are constantly critical. There is an ancient Greek legend about the god Monas. He had a reputation among the other gods for being a constant critic. One day the gods had a competition to see who could make something really special. One of them made a man – and Monas criticised it because it didn't have a window in the front so that he could see what the man was thinking. Another built a superb house – and Monas criticised it because it didn't have wheels so that it could be moved to another location. Another of the gods made a bull – and Monas criticised it too; he said the horns should be below the eyes so that it could see what it was goring. And at the end of the competition Monas got the boot out of heaven! He was banished to a domain of his own where he could criticise himself as much as he wanted to!

The order of the boot would be a good thing for some of us when we get into our 'moany' mood! How much easier it is to do a demolition job on someone's personality and character than it is to build them up. You've probably seen clips of film on TV which show a crowd of people standing at a safe distance from a tall building. Someone presses a button and there's a huge explosion. In a moment a block of flats twenty storeys high is reduced to a pile of rubble. It takes about ten seconds for the dust to clear – and then the building is gone. It took a great deal longer to put it up! You and I are guilty sometimes of being demolition experts on people's characters, personality and reputation, even in the life of the church. We are far more likely to point the finger of accusation than to reach out the hand of love; more likely to condemn than to congratulate.

What did Jesus mean by saying, 'in the same way you judge others, you will be judged'? Probably without exception, each time we point a nagging, critical finger at someone else, we are condemning something we have done ourselves. Within days – even minutes – of accusing someone of a fault, we are doing exactly the same thing. We come under our own judgment. 'OK, you think that's wrong?' asks Jesus, 'Well, that condemns you, too, doesn't it?'

There are sometimes masquerade balls on television. A man comes in wearing a mask on both sides of his head – a frowning face on one side and a smiling face on the back, so you can't tell if he's coming or going, or whether you're talking to his face or his back!

We are like that when we make ourselves judges of others. From the front we may look like the judge, wearing his wig and spectacles, but when people see us from the back they see the defendant in the dock.

In God's eyes, whenever we set ourselves up as judge, he sees us as the defendant.

Destructive criticism achieves nothing. It only destroys and hurts, and condemns the critic. Next time you feel like letting off steam about someone – perhaps a work colleague, a family member, a next-door neighbour or your house group leader – stop to ask yourself these questions:

- What will I achieve by saying those critical things?
- How have I been guilty of doing exactly the same thing, though perhaps in a different situation?
- What is there to praise about this person, even about the thing that I was going to criticise?
- What can I say or do to encourage this person?
- If the thing I'm condemning is really important – if it's harming that person's ministry or destroying someone else – when am I going to make time to talk to that person about it face-to-face?

DELUDED CRITICISM

> 'Why do you look at the speck of sawdust in your brother's eye and pay no attention to the plank in your own eye? How can you say to your brother, "Let me take the speck out of your eye," when all the time there is a plank in your own eye? You hypocrite, first take the plank out of your own eye, and then you will see clearly to remove the speck from your brother's eye.' *Matthew 7:3–5*

You know how painful and irritating it can be to get even the smallest speck of dust in your eye. You certainly know about it; it hurts! You want to get it out as soon as you can. But you can't, there isn't a mirror around and you need help. Then along comes a do-gooder who immediately spots your problem. He knows all about this sort of problem; he's dealt with it before. Lots of people suffer from it, but you're OK now because he will sort you out.

I can imagine all the self-made counsellors in Jesus' congregation sitting there nodding wisely. 'Yes, that's my particular gift – sorting people out, fixing their problems.' And then he shows them the rest of the picture. The counsellor heading for 'the person with the problem' has an enormous great plank sticking out of his eye! It's so big it covers both eyes. But he stumbles on towards the horrified victim, tweezers at the ready.

You must understand, says Jesus, how much you need forgiving and sorting out yourself; how much you need to put yourselves right with God before you dare presume to set yourself up as the person with all the answers.

Four things need to happen if we are to stop deluding ourselves about our own condition and that of others:

- We need to get right with God. We can be living on such a 'low' spiritual level that almost all our judgments are suspect. We need to bring ourselves into God's searching gaze, asking for him to show us *our* faults and problems, and seek his forgiveness and help in putting things right.
- We must find out the facts. Before so much as frowning, let alone expressing an opinion, we must find

out the facts. As the pastor of a church, many people have come to me with a criticism of someone else in the church. It is right to share with our church leaders our concerns about others. But in all the cases I have been brought, not a single 'concerned critic' has known all the facts. People have pointed the finger of criticism at someone, not having a clue about the enormous pressures and hurt that person was suffering, and that were making him behave so unpredictably. We can only find out the facts by talking with the person concerned.

• We must find out the feelings. Once we know the facts, we need to go further and try to feel how this person feels. What's eating away at him? Is he feeling depressed? Hopeless? Lonely? A failure? The French have a proverb: 'To know all is to forgive all' – perhaps not entirely true but it takes us a long way towards the truth. When we can stand in someone else's shoes and begin to imagine how his situation must feel, we will find that we are much less eager to judge and condemn.

This was what the incarnation meant for Jesus. God didn't stay up in heaven and bellow out his verdict on us. He came down to walk in our shoes, to live as we live, to experience all the pains and pressures of human life, with parents who didn't understand him and with friends who deserted him. That same principle needs to be worked out in our lives before we get involved in criticising others.

• We must act with compassion. 'Praying' Hyde was a missionary in India. One day he heard a bad report about a fellow evangelist, which incensed him. He immediately got down on his knees (which was his habit – hence his nickname), and said, 'Lord, I want to pray about this man because his faith is so . . .' He was about to say '. . . cold', but before he could get the word out God spoke into his own heart like an arrow. 'Who are you accusing of being cold? Think about what that man has given up for me.' And as 'Praying' Hyde thought about it God reminded him of all that his fellow evangelist had given up to obey God's call: money, job, prestige, status, contacts. And he thought back to all the things God had done through the life and ministry of that man. Then he felt God saying to him, 'Now praise me for all those things.' So he began to pray, 'Lord, thank you for what you did through this man in Bombay, thank you for what you did in Calcutta . . . I praise you for this man's life.'

When he had finished praying, Hyde travelled nearly 100 miles to the village where that man was holding a mission. To Hyde's astonishment, he came running to meet him and said, 'It's great to see you! I must tell you about the things God has been doing in my life this week. I've been feeling so cold recently in my spiritual life and I've found it really difficult to keep going. But this week God has been doing a fresh thing in my life; he's been real to me in such a powerful way!'

Our perception of a situation might be accurate, but there are two ways of responding to it. As Hyde focused on the positive things about the person of whom he was critical, so God worked supernaturally in that person's life to reinforce those good things and to cause the coldness to wither away. God acted with compassion, to change and improve the situation. So should we.

DISCERNING CRITICISM

It is not always right to respond when asked for our opinion or judgment. I was once involved in a mission where we went into the local pubs to talk to people there, on their own home territory. On one occasion I was approached at the bar by someone with a slight stagger, who demanded, 'Tell me about this Jesus, then.' And I said, 'No.' I simply refused to talk to him. But wasn't I on an evangelistic mission? Yes, but I didn't feel it right to talk to this particular, inebriated person about Jesus, when all I had heard from him throughout the rest of the evening was foul-mouthed obscenities and blasphemy. I was not prepared to put Jesus to further shame and mocking from someone who was not going to take the conversation seriously.

It is sometimes the case, of course, that when people mock and criticise our faith they are hiding a deep hurt inside and it would be right to share the gospel with them. But not always. We need to be discerning:

> 'Do not give dogs what is sacred; do not throw your pearls to pigs. If you do, they may trample them under their feet, and then turn and tear you to pieces.'
>
> *Matthew 7:6*

How can we know when it might be right or wrong to speak out, whether in constructive criticism or in sharing the gospel? Here are four things that will help us make wise decisions.

- Get God's view. Most of us base our criticisms on things that have affected us personally. Perhaps we have been offended, hurt, or our values have been challenged.

God asks us to look beyond all that and ask, 'What do *you* think about this, God?' Unlike us, God hasn't had his illusions about that particular person shattered; he didn't have any illusions about her in the first place but has always known the whole truth. His view of her is the only fair one, so we need his mind on the situation, not just our own limited perspective.

- Be repentant. Each of us is guilty of being critical of others without a cause. We need to confess our guilt to God. That's not easy. Most of us are no better than our children when it comes to saying sorry.

'Say you're sorry.'
'Sorry . . . grrrrrrr.'
'Say it!'
'Sorry.'
'Now mean it . . .!'

Unless we are humble enough to apologise to God, making no excuses for ourselves, we cannot move on from simply not criticising to being positive encouragements to one another. It is repentance – painful, and perhaps with tears – that breaks us of the desire to carry on doing what is wrong. Without this 'cleaning up' process there can be no healthy new life. It's like a visit to the dentist when you have toothache. As he reaches across for the dreaded drill you suddenly have a good idea: 'Tell you what, how about just filling the tooth – it would save all that drilling time!' 'Sorry,' would be his response, 'no drilling, no filling.' God cannot build good things in our lives on rotten foundations. Without our repentance, how can God's blessing follow?

- Go to the source, the person concerned. Most of us have shared our grievance with at least five people before we think about talking to the person who caused us all this bother in the first place! That's basically because we are cowards, or because we don't really want to confront the situation. Our concern isn't really to put things right, but to enjoy a good moan or a wallow in self-pity. If our first move is to talk to the person concerned, that will probably be the only move we need make.

- Cultivate the positive. We must learn to be builders, not demolishers. God is at work in the lives of each of his children to build them up and display more of his kingdom glory in them. But if we are criticising and tearing down those people, we are working against God, setting ourselves up in opposition to him. He calls us to give all that we have and are to him for his use – and that includes our tongues and our critical faculties. So let us use them to do his work.

10

PERSISTENCE

I am indebted to my young daughter for having given me a new perspective on what can easily become a routine: Sunday worship. One Sunday morning I was in the shower when Bethany came into the bathroom and yanked back the shower curtain – always a messy business. And as she stood there she asked, 'Daddy, do you want to go to church this morning?' I thought about that for a moment and said, 'Yes! Yes, I really do want to go to church this morning!' And I became quite excited by the prospect and started singing in the shower about how good it is to be able to worship God and pray to him.

We don't always feel like that. But whether we feel glad to be worshipping God or feel it's a real drag, it's still right to do it. Someone once asked Spurgeon, 'When should I pray? Should I pray when I don't feel like it?' He answered, 'Pray when you feel like it, because God will bless you; pray when you don't feel like it, because that's when you most need it.'

Jesus laid a great deal of stress on the importance of 'keeping on', of persisting in our walk with God. In his sermon he outlines four major areas where we need to 'keep on keeping on' if we are to get anywhere worthwhile.

PERSISTENT PRAYER

> 'Ask and it will be given to you; seek and you will find; knock and the door will be opened to you. For everyone who asks receives; he who seeks finds; and to him who knocks, the door will be opened.'
>
> *Matthew 7:7–8*

We are to keep on asking, seeking and knocking. If, at home, you say to your child, 'Pick up that pencil you've just dropped on the floor,' that's a 'one off' command. You don't mean 'keep on picking up that pencil and putting it back on the floor, then picking it up again.'

But if the child goes out of the room leaving the door wide open and you say, 'When you leave the room, please shut the door,' you mean that in a more general sense. In other words, 'Every time you go out of the room or come in, please don't forget to close the door behind you.'

It's in the second sense that Jesus speaks of asking, seeking and knocking on God's door in prayer.

Prayer that keeps going

Much of my prayer life is very weak. One day I'll feel compelled to pray about an issue, but the next day I may have forgotten it.

In 1836 George Müller opened an orphanage for children in Bristol. He and his wife had no resources with which to run it, so each day he would pray for whatever they needed. He would pray very specifically: 'Lord, in the morning we will need three pints of milk and two loaves of bread.' And, come the morning, there would be on the doorstep exactly three pints of milk and two loaves of bread. God answered those prayers in a remarkable way. Yet the same man was also praying for something else. Each day he would pray for the conversion of a particular friend of his and that friend's son. He prayed for that friend for over forty years! When Müller died, his friend still had not been converted. But God honoured his prayer and responded to it in his own timing: Müller's friend was converted while attending his funeral, and the friend's son a week later.

His prayers were effective because he was determined not to let anything knock him sideways in his prayer life or stop him being committed to something. What were you praying about last week? Last month? Last year? What were the matters burning in your mind? Have those prayers been answered? If not, perhaps you should still be persisting in bringing them to God.

Prayer that isn't a slave to 'fashion'

Part of the problem is that we are so fashion-conscious in our prayers. Ethiopia is 'in' for a month or two; then it goes out of fashion as Romania takes the stage. Then that's 'out' and the Gulf War is 'in'. But people are still dying in Ethiopia; orphanages in Romania are still desperately under-equipped; and refugees from the Gulf War continue to struggle for survival.

Let me pull another name out of the pack: Biafra.

The plight of Biafran refugees is still as awful as it was when they were hot news. But they are no longer 'media-worthy' so they drop out of our thinking. We need to be consistent as well as persistent in our praying. Keep a note book of topics and names of people that you feel you should pray for. Update it from time to time, and keep at it!

PERSISTENT TRUST

> 'Which of you, if his son asks for bread, will give him a stone? Or if he asks for a fish, will give him a snake? If you, then, though you are evil, know how to give good gifts to your children, how much more will your Father in heaven give good gifts to those who ask him!'
>
> *Matthew 7:9–11*

When God doesn't seem to be hearing or answering our prayers, our trust in his goodness or willingness to answer can waver. 'Don't let it,' Jesus says. God really is hearing and is concerned.

Colin Urquart tells a story about a time when he was on a flight home to England from Australia. With every meal on that flight, he was served orange juice, until he was absolutely fed up with it. So he said, 'Lord, I'd give anything not to have orange juice with the next meal; please could I have something else?' And when the stewardesses came round again, they served him pineapple juice! He said he was so thrilled it seemed like the best answer to prayer he'd ever had!

That was such a small thing, but our heavenly Father is interested in every little detail of our lives. He wants to listen to us, but sometimes we are so unready to ask. So what happens when our prayers don't seem to be answered? Is God sitting up there making fun of our puny requests? No, far from it. Jesus looked around at the crowds and asked which human father would do that to his child. If their child asked for a little round, flat loaf of bread, would any father give him a little round, flat stone instead? It would look just like the loaf of bread, and would shut the child up for a while. But it would be a cruel father who could watch his child bite into it and break his teeth.

God is nothing like that. He longs to give us good things. He loves it when we are happy. When we are thrilled with his gifts, he is delighted! I love giving treats to my young daughters. Chocolate buttons are their favourite. I'll line up the buttons on the armchair at home and the girls will stand there, poised, looking up at me. Then I'll ask, 'What do you say?' 'Please!' comes the reply. 'OK.' And if I don't stop them they'll go down the line of buttons as fast as they can, cramming them into their mouths.

What I really enjoy is seeing their faces light up just as they are about to launch into the chocolate. They're so good to be nice to, because they get excited about it! If I say to them, 'Do you want some buttons?' they dance on the spot with joy! By comparison, people can do the greatest favours for us – and we're 'flat' and unresponsive.

Our heavenly Father longs to give us good gifts. Sometimes when I'm praying I hear an accusing voice in my head saying, 'God's not going to answer *that* prayer; you don't need that, you just want it!' Well, great! God sometimes does give us things we don't need but simply want, because he is a God of bounty and excess. He is the God who fed 5000 people and had enough left to set someone up in their own catering business. He didn't skimp on it, saying, 'There's just enough here for the picnic, folks; can you go easy on it, please.'

'Ask, and you will receive,' he says. 'I long to pour out my blessings on you.' Let's take him at his word and not doubt his love, his good intentions for us, or his generosity.

PERSISTENT SELFLESSNESS

> 'In everything, do to others what you would have them do to you, for this sums up the Law and the Prophets.'
>
> *Matthew 7:12*

This saying of Jesus has become world famous as 'the golden rule'. The surprising thing is that before Jesus did so, no one had put that thought in the positive. The Jews knew the principle, it was stated in their Law, but it was put negatively: 'Don't do to others what you wouldn't like them to do to you.' Jesus cast that command in a totally new light by restating it positively.

There's a story of two famous rabbis who lived in New Testament times not long after Jesus. One was a mean old grouch and the other was a really approachable sort of guy. A Gentile came up to the mean old grouch and said, 'If the Jewish faith is so significant, tell me what it's all about, quickly. If you can sum it up in just a few minutes – while I'm standing on one leg – I'll believe you.' And the rabbi said, grouchily, 'Go away. I can't possibly do that.'

Then the Gentile went to the other rabbi. 'Tell me all about the Jewish faith,' he asked. 'And tell me while I'm standing on one leg.' And, quick as anything, the rabbi responded, 'Do to others what you would have them do to you. Everything else is commentary. Bye!'

This second rabbi had got to the heart of the Jewish law. And Jesus brought out that teaching clearly. Yet we Christians seem to have forgotten the practice of this 'golden rule'. How much of what I've said privately in the past week would have been said if my life had been governed by this rule? How many people have I let down in the past month because I didn't do something I said I would – and it was something important to them?

The reason why we have probably lost sight of this rule is that it sounds so 'unspiritual'. For one thing it's a 'rule', and we're into grace, not law. For another, it sounds as if we're trying to earn God's approval by being do-gooders. For a third, shouldn't we be more concerned about preaching the gospel to people than with being nice to them? These are all false distinctions. True spirituality will show itself in the way we love, care for and respect other people. The way to ensure that we're doing that to the best of our Spirit-filled ability is to try to put this rule into practice.

PERSISTENT DISCIPLESHIP

> 'Enter through the narrow gate. For wide is the gate and broad is the road that leads to destruction, and many enter through it. But small is the gate and narrow the road that leads to life, and only a few find it.'
>
> *Matthew 7:13–14*

This is the crunch point of Jesus' sermon; it's make-your-mind-up time. Jesus is looking for one hundred per cent commitment. There can be no half measures. We are either in the kingdom of God or in the kingdom of Satan. In wartime you can't be on both sides at once.

Disciples whose commitment is total

Jesus sums up the whole of his sermon in this stark either-or statement. There is a narrow way – do you want to choose it? That's the way of the beatitudes, being single-minded in our longing for God, putting into practice all that teaching about the Law, living a life of transparent integrity, clearing out the grime and dirt from the cellars of our lives, living by that clear, unbending 'golden rule'. There is also a broad way – it's much easier, you just do what comes naturally.

The broad way seems sensible and obvious. That's why so many people are on it. At work or with our friends the question will arise time and again in our minds, 'Why shouldn't I do it? Everyone else is.' 'Why shouldn't I take that from the store cupboard at work? Everyone else does. Why shouldn't I use language like that? All my mates do. Why shouldn't I cheat on my wife? Everyone does that sort of thing.'

Actually, there are some people living differently. Jesus invites you to join them – a group of people who, down through history, have either been persecuted or labelled 'oddballs' because of it. 'You need to choose,' says Jesus. 'I invite you to join me, to choose a life that is tough and demanding, that will take your total commitment, but that will also be deeply satisfying and have eternal value.'

Many of us have made that decision. We have taken Jesus up on his challenge and have committed ourselves to him for life. And yet there are still those pockets of resistance in our lives, areas where we have not allowed him to take control.

During the American Civil War, Abraham Lincoln met with the generals of the Southern armies on a number of occasions as the war progressed, to seek a peaceful end to it. The Southerners wanted to keep on these meetings because they were getting fairly profoundly bashed up. After one year of war they came to Lincoln and said, 'OK, we'll give in. Just let us have Texas, New Mexico, the southern bit of California and one or two other States. You can have everything else.' And Lincoln refused. Another year went by and the Southerners became more desperate. 'How about letting us have just Texas and New Mexico? The North can keep everything else.' Abraham Lincoln reached over the table, put his hand on the map of the whole of America and said, 'Gentlemen, this Government wants it all.' Then he left the negotiating table and refused to meet with his opponents again until they came back in unconditional surrender.

While we carry on trying to keep some sovereign States in our lives apart from God, he is unable to give us all that he longs to. He cannot fill us with himself or direct us fully, because there is civil war going on inside us. God is putting his hand on the map of our lives and saying, 'My Government wants it all. Not just the bits you feel you can spare; not some bits and not others; I want all of your life.'

Disciples who are mature

> 'Watch out for false prophets. They come to you in sheep's clothing, but inwardly they are ferocious wolves. By their fruit you will recognise them. Do people pick grapes from thornbushes, or figs from thistles? Likewise every good tree bears good fruit, but a bad tree bears bad fruit. A good tree cannot bear bad fruit, and a bad tree cannot bear good fruit. Every tree that does not bear good fruit is cut down and thrown into the fire. Thus, by their fruit you will recognise them.
>
> *Matthew 7:15–20*

As Jesus comes to the end of his sermon, he sees how the crowd has swelled in size. There are disciples, half-disciples, the vaguely interested, and their friends, families, cousins, aunties and uncles. They are fascinated by his revolutionary teaching. He acknowledges the interest and attentiveness with which they hear him and he gives them a glimpse of the future. Yes, he says, his teaching is good and true, and many in those crowds will become his disciples. But there will come a time when those who recognise the power of his teaching will want the power without the teaching. They will want for themselves the devotion Jesus' disciples are to give to him alone. They will be false prophets and teachers, wolves in sheep's clothing – the exact opposite of what they purport to be.

His words have proved to be true. Down through history, from the time of the first apostles, false teachers have done all they can to distort the truth and the minds of God's people, so that our walk with God is not an easy one. We are constantly presented with new ideas, more 'intellectually acceptable' ideas about the resurrection of Jesus, for instance; highways and byways to go wandering into, attractive-looking cul-de-sacs down which to walk.

Individual church fellowships are particularly prone to drifting into heresy, especially when they have a strong leader with no one seriously disputing what he decrees. A group known as the Children of God grew out of the Jesus movement of the 1960s and 1970s. They were a great bunch of people, sharing their faith warmly and openly on the streets and attracting many people to Christ. But where are they now? Under a strong leader, who calls himself Moses David, they have become a cult which is into 'prostitution', fund-raising, subversive high-pressure activity and gross distortion of the gospel message – all within just a few years.

Today in America, those who teach a 'prosperity gospel' are also, I believe, heading towards cultism. They teach that God loves us – yes, and that he wants the best for us – yes; so we should ask him for what we want: 'name it and claim it' is their slogan. If you want a Mercedes, ask God for it! If you've got enough faith, God will give it to you. Of course, if you don't get one, that shows there's something wrong in your life or with your prayers or faith. Well, if they're right, I obviously don't have a very good prayer life!

Satan is cunning in the way he entices us to swallow lies like this. He doesn't come straight out with rubbish or heresy; he latches on to a particular biblical truth, and then pushes it beyond the limits it was meant to go. He takes a single truth and blows it out of proportion or corrupts it in some other way. It sounds so logical and right, to begin with. And then you get involved with a closely knit group of people and give its leader your loyalty. And then it is very hard to disentangle yourself. Any hint of dissent is condemned as being unspiritual and rebellious. You just can't win in that sort of set-up. The wolves have got you fairly cornered.

It is crucial to know our Bibles and be able to test against its teaching the teaching of groups and sects we come across. But another test to apply is the fruit test: what are these people's lives like? Do they display the fruit of the Spirit? Do they uphold the great biblical moral values – chastity outside marriage, faithfulness within it, honesty and integrity in every aspect of life? Does their theology lead them to live Christ-like lives?

Jesus doesn't leave things here. It is easy enough to apply these tests to other people and denounce those we find to be at fault. But he suddenly makes things very personal.

Disciples who love their Lord

> 'Not everyone who says to me, "Lord, Lord," will enter the kingdom of heaven, but only he who does the will of my Father who is in heaven. Many will say to me on that day, "Lord, Lord, did we not prophesy in your name, and in your name drive out demons and perform many miracles?" Then I will tell them plainly, "I never knew you. Away from me, you evildoers!" ' *Matthew 7:21–23*

I don't know about you, but I would be delighted to be able to stand in God's presence and say, 'Lord, I've cast out lots of demons, I've worked hundreds of miracles, and I simply couldn't stop prophesying!' To you and I, people who could truly stand up and say that would seem like spiritual giants, capable of anything in the realm of spiritual battle. Yet Jesus is going to say he never knew them. I find that amazing. What is he wanting us to learn from it? This: that it is obedience he has in store for his people, not simply the miraculous.

It is right that we look for the exorcism of demons, where that is appropriate, for miracles and for prophesy. But the ability to do those things is not the ultimate test of a person's walk with God. There is great danger in judging either our own spiritual standing or that of others on the evidence of what we can see, rather than on what is unseen. The wolves in sheep's clothing look very much like the real thing on the outside, but inside they are very different. We might look very spiritual on the outside, but God knows whether our heart is right with him.

Many of us think, 'I know I've been saved by grace but, my word, God is going to be really grateful to me when I get to heaven because I've done quite a few good things!' When I get to the pearly gates, God isn't going to bring out a great check-list of things and tick off all those things I've accomplished in my life. The test is going to be, did I love Jesus and follow him? And whatever was apparent to people on the outside who looked on, was there a deep, God-given integrity about my life? Or did I say one thing in public and do another in private? Did I urge people to spend time in prayer and reading the word of God, while neglecting to do so myself? Did I encourage people to share their faith, while having none to share myself?

Performance, skill, gifts, abilities – without inner integrity all these things are ultimately of no use to us. What counts for eternity is a heart that is right with King Jesus.

11

BUILDING ON SOLID GROUND

I recently read the book *Spy Catcher*, by Peter Wright. In it he reveals an astounding level of lack of trust, lying, deceit and intrigue within the Secret Services and the world of politics. He portrays a world where you simply do not know who you can trust, who your friends are, or what you can say to whom. He shows a world where everyone is constantly watching their backs, constantly living 'on edge'.

In a smaller, less potent way, all our lives can be like that – looking over our shoulders, wondering who we can trust with a problem, which of our friends are genuine and which are simply fair-weather friends. We're always searching for a foundational security that will not waver or fail. Where can we find that?

> ' "Therefore, everyone who hears these words of mine and puts them into practice is like a wise man who built his house on the rock. The rain came down, the streams rose, and the winds blew and beat against that house; yet it did not fall, because it had its foundation on the rock. But everyone who hears these words of mine and does not put them into practice is like a foolish man who built his

> house on sand. The rain came down, the streams rose, and the winds blew and beat against that house, and it fell with a great crash."
>
> When Jesus had finished saying these things, the crowds were amazed at his teaching, because he taught as one who had authority, and not as their teachers of the law.'
>
> *Matthew 7:24–29*

Jesus asks some hard questions! Behind his words here are the questions, 'What do you want to build your life on? What really matters to you? What are you going to give your life for and to?' If we're building on something insubstantial, the whole edifice of our lives is likely to come crumbling down around us. On the other hand, if our life is built on values that hold good through all eternity, then what we build on them will last too.

What will you find when you get to the top of your particular ladder? That it was leaning against the wrong wall all those years? All the money you earned, all the status and success you achieved – was it all worth while? What a tragedy to get to the end of life only to discover that it was just one big waste of time.

Jesus offers us a rock-like foundation on which to build; something that will give strength to all that we build on it and stay firm through the bad times as well as the good. He says, 'These words of mine, these are the foundational facts on which you need to build your life. Everything else is useless and insubstantial. If you build on anything else, you're wasting your time.'

How do we go about building on Jesus' words? There are two things we must do:

Hear God's word

Speaking in this passage, Jesus was referring primarily to his sermon, but we need to go on hearing God's word if we are to build our lives on what he says. God wants to speak to us in our reading of the Bible, in our prayer life, as we talk with other Christians and listen to his word being proclaimed from the pulpit. So we need to make the time to hear him in all these ways.

We can easily fall into the habit of tuning God out, developing a screening system that prevents us listening to anything we might find challenging or uncomfortable. Perhaps I've decided that my house group leader isn't able to tell me anything I don't already know, so I turn up at house group with my ears firmly closed to anything God might want to say through him. We can be prejudiced about other Christians, through whom God might want to speak to us. They're 'too young in the faith' to be able to teach me anything, or they're really a bit thick. And God certainly wouldn't teach me anything through a woman, would he?'

When my wife asks Cara to put away the toys, Cara takes not a blind bit of notice. She has perfected the art of tuning out whatever she doesn't want to hear. She'll actually turn her head away when asked to tidy up, as if to prove that her ears don't exist! Jan sometimes has to get hold of her by the chin and turn her round to face her, saying, 'Look at me when I'm talking to you!' She demands that Cara comes out of her little world and listens.

We've muddled along in our Christian lives for long enough. God longs for our attention so that he can say something to us. He wants to take hold of our chins and turn us to look at him and listen to him, so that he can change us and give us the power to be different.

Obey God's word

I was marrying a couple in church and had got to the point where you look the groom straight in the eye and say, 'Will you take this woman to be your lawful wedded wife?' And you expect the quick response, 'I will.' Now this particular couple both affirmed that boldly, but if the groom had hesitated I'd probably have said the words again, in case he'd not heard. And if he'd whispered back, 'I'm thinking about it', I'd have got pretty worried! He'd planned for this marriage for ages: asked the bride, asked the bride's parents, got all the arrangements done, and arrived at the front of the church with all their relatives looking on. All that he needed to make the marriage happen was to say the words, 'I will.' All of his previous promises to his fiancée would have been seen as so much twaddle if he hadn't carried it through to its legal conclusion.

Many of us have made all sorts of promises to God. We tell him that we want to do this and that for him, serve him and obey him, but when it comes to the crunch we are very bad at carrying through on those promises. There is a cost to building on solid, secure, reliable foundations. And that cost is obedience to God's word.

What is your life being built on? At the end, when you stand on the threshold of eternity, will you look back on it and see a wonderful edifice crumble to nothing before your eyes as the sand beneath it shifts and blows away? Or will you be able to look back and see something of lasting worth and value, built through obedience on the rock-hard foundation of God's word?

OTHER BOOKS IN THIS SERIES

Pioneers or Settlers? Exodus: Adventurous faith for today (Philip Mohabir).

God of New Beginnings: Matthew 1–4 in today's world (Roger Sainsbury).

Drawing Power: Living out Acts in today's world (Derek Prime).

Growing your Gifts: 2 Timothy: Ministry in today's world (Stephen Gaukroger).